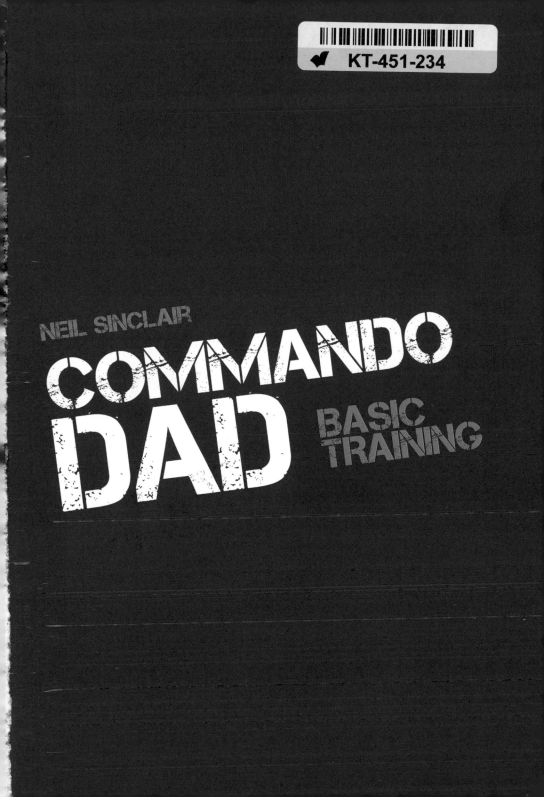

NEIL SINCLAIR

COMMANDO
DAD

BASIC
TRAINING

COMMANDO DAD: BASIC TRAINING

Vie Books is an imprint of Summersdale Publishers Ltd

An Hachette UK Company
www.hachette.co.uk

Summersdale Publishers Ltd
Part of Octopus Publishing Group Limited
Carmelite House
50 Victoria Embankment
LONDON
EC4Y 0DZ
UK

www.summersdale.com

Printed and bound in the Czech Republic

ISBN: 978-1-84953-261-7

Substantial discounts on bulk quantities of Summersdale books are available to corporations, professional associations and other organisations. For details contact general enquiries: telephone: +44 (0) 1243 771107 or email: enquiries summersdale.com.

DISCLAIMER
The information given in this book should not be treated as a substitute for qualified medical advice; always consult a medical practitioner. Neither the author nor the publisher can be held responsible for any loss or claim arising out of the use, or misuse, of the suggestions made or the failure to take medical advice.

The intent of the author is only to offer information of a general nature to help you to gain competence as a parent.

NEIL SINCLAIR

COMMANDO DAD
BASIC TRAINING

HOW TO BE AN ELITE DAD OR CARER

FROM BIRTH TO 3 YEARS

Foreword by Dr Jan Mager-Jones MB ChB

CONTENTS

FOREWORD

By Dr Jan Mager-Jones MB ChB

For most couples, bringing a baby home from hospital is the exciting start of a new life as parents. However, it is easy to feel completely overwhelmed by the enormous sense of responsibility for this new little life and those first days and weeks bring with them the realisation that suddenly every task seems to require incredible organisational skills; looking after a baby or young child is almost like a military operation!!

Neil Sinclair knows all about military operations having served as a Royal Engineer Commando. When he exchanged his military life for the role of stay-at-home-dad, he realised how important it was to have an accessible reference manual.

Commando Dad: Basic Training is a fantastic new parenting manual which provides just that. It is concise and small enough to carry with you, but contains a wealth of step-by-step instructions for everything you need to do for your baby and toddler. The novel presentation in the style of a military handbook makes it a fun read, whilst providing simple, clear guidance for everything from preparing base camp (getting everything ready at home prior to the baby's arrival) to bomb disposal (getting rid of dirty nappies!).

As a family doctor I frequently see new mums and dads who feel the pressures of parenthood, and with teenage boys of my own the memories are not too distant of how challenging it can be. I highly recommend this great new manual, which I can imagine being a well-thumbed and much-loved addition to every new dad's back pocket.

This book is dedicated to my own amazing unit: my wife, Tara, and our three troopers, Sam, Jude and Liberty. It is also for all the dads who kept asking, 'Have you written that book yet? I really need a copy.'

Thank you all.

Author's note

I am a stay-at-home Commando Dad and registered childminder, and have personally tried and tested all of the techniques outlined in this basic training manual. Where I mention anything to do with the health and safety of your troopers, I have had the text reviewed and approved by a health-care professional with a view to making sure that the information contained in the book is accurate and in keeping with current thinking and practice at the time of publication. However, the publisher, authors and experts disclaim any liability from any injury that may result from the use, proper or improper, of the information contained in this book. Guidance and guidelines on baby care change constantly and *Commando Dad: Basic Training* should not be considered a substitute for the advice of your health-care professional or your own common sense.

Content has been approved by:
Rachel Jessey, Nutritional Therapist DipCNM mBANT www.benourished.co.uk
Sally Jordan RGN and Health Visitor
Dr Jan Mager-Jones MB ChB
Damon Marriott, Approved Child Safety Advisor for the Britax Excellence Centre

With thanks to Sarah Thorsby.

INTRODUCTION

TO ALL DADS AND CARERS (henceforth known as '**Commando Dads**')

This book has been written for YOU.

I have been a Royal Engineer Commando, a Physical Education teacher, a security guard at the UK Mission to the UN in New York, a stay-at-home dad and a registered childminder, and I can honestly tell you that there have been few times in my life as daunting as bringing my first son back from the hospital.

All the parenting books and classes were geared towards the birth, and then suddenly you and your partner find yourselves back at home with the baby. In charge.

I found myself thinking how much easier life would be if I had been issued with a basic training manual for my little baby trooper (henceforth referred to as BT), like the manual you get when you join the army. Any soldier will tell you that one of the greatest weapons in their armoury is Basic Battle Skills: a 'How To' training manual handed to them on day one as a soldier. It covers everything from how to shave to how to accurately estimate the distance to a target, and provides the foundation to all the practical skills needed to become a first-rate soldier.

I did try and find such a manual, but the books available for new dads were either novelty books (and believe me, gentlemen, if your parenting is a laugh a minute, you're doing it wrong) or, even worse, books that were too wordy to be practical. At 0-silly-hundred-hours, with a screaming BT in your arms, 700 pages of someone telling you about their emotions isn't the answer.

I decided that what I needed was an accessible basic training manual for parents and, more specifically, dads.

Gentlemen, in your hands you are holding that manual.

Emotions are important. But within seconds of the birth of your trooper you will know how you *feel*. I felt love, fear, confusion, frustration and awe, and that was within the first hour. This book is intended to help you know what to *do*.

As a basic training manual, *Commando Dad* can only take you so far though. The rest is up to you. To be an effective dad you need to supplement this manual with a lot of practical experience. You need to step up, get out there and do it. This brings me to the first rule of being a Commando Dad:

★ ★ ★

A COMMANDO DAD IS A HANDS-ON DAD

It won't feel like it now, but you have an unbelievably short time with your troopers. There aren't even 2,000 days between birth and age five, when your trooper starts school. In less than 7,000 days from the day they're born, your trooper will be 18.

You may not be the full-time carer for your trooper, you may see them only at weekends or in the evenings, you may not be their biological dad, but none of that matters. What matters is that you make the time you spend together really count. And the best way to do that is to apply military precision to your parenting.

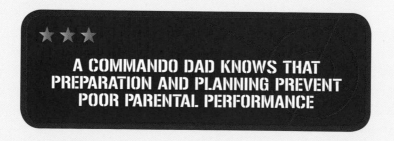

★ ★ ★

A COMMANDO DAD KNOWS THAT PREPARATION AND PLANNING PREVENT POOR PARENTAL PERFORMANCE

Take pride in your unit. Reduce unnecessary stress and worry by gaining confidence in your own skills. Be prepared. Act in a way befitting your Commando Dad status. You may not find it easy – but then nothing worth doing is ever easy.

To a child, a dad has many roles, often falling somewhere between Hero, Role Model and Protector. You are now stepping into those shoes. You owe it to yourself – and your troopers – to be the best dad that you can be. *Right now*. Let training commence.

How to use *Commando Dad: Basic Training*

Commando Dad: Basic Training is designed to be used by dads 'in the field' (i.e. while you are actively engaged in parenting manoeuvres), so I have taken a lot of care to pack essential information into a book that will comfortably fit into your pocket.

There is a fully interactive website that provides essential backup support to *Commando Dad: Basic Training*: www.commandodad.com. Throughout the book you will be directed there to find out more information on everything from the different types of nappies available to where to find extra resources on nutrition and getting your BT to sleep. It features short, practical 'how to' videos on essential skills such as holding, bathing and burping your BT. And the all-important 'How to change a nappy' video too, of course. The site also contains a wealth of other resources that new recruits to fatherhood will find useful. Please log on now to find out what's available, and to join a forum so that you can start sharing your thoughts with me and other Commando Dads.

Throughout *Commando Dad: Basic Training* I use military terminology, and also terms that I have invented in my years as a Commando Dad. I include a glossary at the end of every chapter to explain specific terms used.

By far the most important terms in the book are:

- BT: baby trooper. A trooper (child) before it is mobile.
- MT: mobile trooper. A trooper that can shuffle, crawl, stand up and, eventually, walk.

When I refer to 'troopers' I use it in the generic sense of 'children'.

I also use 'Common Sense' icons as well as diagrams throughout *Commando Dad: Basic Training*. This is designed to make the book as accessible (and less wordy) as possible.

CHAPTER 1:
THE ADVANCE PARTY: PREPARING BASE CAMP

The brief:
Your life is about to change beyond all recognition. Do as much preparation beforehand as possible to save yourself precious time and energy: both will be in short supply in the months to come.

Objective:
By the end of today's briefing you will have a greater understanding of:

- How to prepare base camp for your BT.
- The essentials you need in preparation for bringing your BT back to base camp.
- The essentials you need when bringing your BT home from hospital.

> ★ ★ ★
> ## A COMMANDO DAD KNOWS THAT PREPARATION AND PLANNING PREVENT POOR PARENTAL PERFORMANCE

Around six weeks before your BT is due, start to prepare the base camp. You will need to:

- Clean.
- Plan.
- Prepare.
- Assign specific areas for your BT and their equipment.

Clean

The aim is to thoroughly clean – not sterilise – your BT's environment. It is impossible to eliminate germs completely; you are not running a field hospital. Even if it were possible to create a germ-free environment (it isn't), it would be unsustainable. Use your common sense. Cleaning and tidying as you go along needs to become your new standard operating procedure (SOP).

Clean your BT's room

It is unlikely that your BT will sleep in a room on their own for at least six months after birth. Nevertheless, it is still advisable to do any deep cleaning before they arrive at base camp, while you have the time to do it.

Do:
- Wipe down walls.
- Clean carpets and rugs.
- Dust and polish.

Don't:
- Paint the room the BT will be sleeping in shortly before they come back to base camp. The fumes could be harmful.
- Use harsh chemicals.

Clean surfaces that your BT will come into contact with, including:

- Nursery furniture.
- Changing tables.
- Baby bath.

Always keep your hands clean. Keep nails short and dirt-free.

Plan

Base camp essentials – what you need now

Changing

- Nappies. If using disposable nappies, buy the newborn size and the next size up. BTs grow quickly.
- If using cloth nappies, get up to speed on the different types now. Don't buy too many nappies until you know the weight of your BT. You may find cloth nappies do not suit your lifestyle, so a big up front expenditure on such items could be avoided. For more information on the different types of nappies available, go to *Resources* on www.commandodad.com.
- Baby wipes or cotton wool.
- Nappy-rash cream.
- Changing mat.
- Nappy bags if desired. Useful, but not essential, for 'bomb disposal'. Any small plastic bag will serve as a good alternative if you are out of nappy bags – ideally, a biodegradable one.

Clothing

- 6 x babygros and 6 x sleepsuits with poppers. These are practical, comfortable and easily accessible for changing nappies.
- 6 sets of socks (beware, they will kick them off on a regular basis) for when your BT isn't in a sleepsuit that has feet.
- 3 x pairs of scratch mittens to prevent your BT scratching their own face.
- 3 x cardigans or cotton jackets. Thin layers are better than very thick clothes.
- 3 x cotton hats to keep your BT warm (a lot of heat escapes through the head). If the weather is cold, you will need a soft, warm hat for outdoor wear.
- 2 x baby blankets, sometimes called 'receiving blankets'. These are smaller than cot blankets and are used for keeping your BT warm throughout the day.

Feeding

- If your partner is breastfeeding, a breast pump can be beneficial, as can breast pads and nipple cream.
- If breastfeeding is not an option, bottle feeding is the alternative. Current government recommendations are for mothers to breastfeed where possible.
- 2 x bottles. You will need more (8 is an ideal number to ensure you always have clean bottles) but you need to know if your BT will like the bottle you have chosen. Deciding which bottle and teat to go for is a potential minefield. Arm yourself with more information about what's available by visiting the *Resources* section of www.commandodad.com.
- Spare teats. When you know the bottle your BT will take to, be sure to buy spare teats. Teats that are torn or deteriorated will need to be discarded straight away.
- 2 x bottlebrushes.
- Sterilising equipment of your choice. See *Chapter 2: New Recruits: Surviving the First 24 Hours* for more information on sterilisation equipment.
- An insulated bottle carrier, if required: for times when you are out and about, without access to a cookhouse, and need to give your BT a warm bottle.

Bathing

- Baby bath wash and shampoo, which will be used sparingly. Buy brands that will not sting if they get in the eyes.
- Soft flannels and towels.
- A foam bath-support if required.
- A baby bath.

Sleeping

- Moses basket or cot with a **new**, snug-fitting mattress. Gaps around the mattress can be dangerous. Do not use second-hand mattresses as they may pose a health risk.

- A room thermometer.
- Baby monitors if you wish to use them.

Bedding

- 3 x cot sheets that are either fitted (with elasticated corners) or can be tucked in well.
- 4 x thin, soft cotton blankets and 2 x cellular blankets. Layering blankets will make it easier to regulate your BT's temperature.

First Aid

- Digital ear thermometer.
- Paediatric paracetamol (suitable from two months old) and paediatric ibuprofen (suitable from three months old). Check the label to ensure your BT meets the weight and age requirements. If your BT was premature, count their age from their due date.
- Baby syringe (for administering medicine).
- Antiseptic wipes or alcohol wipes for cleaning the umbilical cord, or stump.

These will supplement the first aid kit, which will contain items such as antiseptic cream, plasters and bandages. See *Chapter 8: Call the Medic: Basic First Aid and Unit Maintenance* for more details.

Transport

Research all transport choices before investing. See *Chapter 10: On Manoeuvres: Transporting the Troops* for advice and tips.

- Car seat that meets safety standards and fits safely and securely in your car. Hand-me-down car seats from older troopers, friends or relatives are fine provided they have never been damaged (or been involved in a car accident). Do not buy a second-hand car seat, or accept one from a relative or friend, unless you can guarantee that this is the case. Also check manufacturer's advice on the correct fitting and the lifespan of the seat, as some recommend not using it after a certain timescale. Never entrust your troopers to an unsafe car seat. The consequences are simply too terrible to contemplate.

- Baby carrier.
- Pushchair. You won't need this straight away.

Nursery Furniture

All furniture can be bought second-hand. If buying new furniture, order for delivery at least a month before your BT is due.

- Comfortable chair (for you to sit in to feed, play and comfort your BT).
- Soft lighting (even if it's just a small bedside lamp with a low-wattage bulb). The 'big light' used in the small hours can startle and stimulate both of you.
- Blackout blinds, or thick curtains.
- Changing table, if required. I preferred to use a mobile changing station, i.e. keeping all my nappy-changing kit mobile and changing my BT/MT on an available stable and safe surface (e.g. the floor or the middle of a bed).

Dummies

Using dummies is a matter of choice – both for you and your BT. My first-born BT rejected the dummy completely. BTs can be given a dummy to comfort them or to help them go to sleep, but try to avoid giving it to them all the time. This will not only reduce its effectiveness as a sleep aid, but also increase your BT's reliance on it. If you do choose to use a dummy, health-care professionals advise the use of orthodontic teats, as they are designed to cause the least damage to the growth of your BTs teeth. For more information about dummies, see *Resources* on www.commandodad.com.

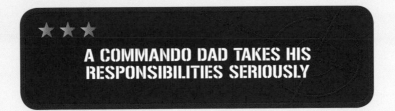

★ ★ ★

A COMMANDO DAD TAKES HIS RESPONSIBILITIES SERIOUSLY

Make your base camp safe

- Install/ check batteries on smoke alarms. The Fire Service will do this free of charge, as well as inspect your home and advise on the best place to fit them.
- Put anti-slip underlay beneath rugs.
- Install a fire extinguisher in the cookhouse.
- Tie up any dangling cords from windows and light switches.
- Put all low-lying items out of reach.

Baby proof your base camp

Not strictly necessary before the BT comes back to base camp, but a base camp recce is recommended now. If base camp is an obstacle course, rearrange it. In the first few weeks you are going to be sleep-deprived and moving around a lot at night.

Commando crawl around on your belly to see first-hand what needs to done. Buy essential items now. These may include:

- Covers for unused plug sockets.
- Protective edges for sharp corners on furniture, such as coffee tables.
- A fireguard is a legal requirement if you have a working fireplace or room heater and your trooper is under eight years old.

The most effective baby proofing in the world, however, is your close supervision.

> # COMMANDO DAD TOP TIP
> Don't fit stair gates too early – unless you need them
> to keep pets away from your BT – as they will become
> another obstacle in the first few weeks.

Prepare

- Assemble, assemble, assemble. Get to grips with nursery furniture and new toys. Learn how to assemble – and disassemble – pushchairs and car seats.

- Buy batteries, and spare batteries. Night lights, bouncers and toys will all require batteries.

- Cook and freeze. Start preparing extra-large meals now and freeze the spare portions. Without time to prepare meals when your BT arrives you may find yourself relying on fast food, which can affect your energy levels and mood. Don't do it. See *Chapter 5: Nutrition: An Army Marches on its Stomach* for sensible options.

- Compile a list of important numbers (your midwife, your health visitor, your doctor, NHS Direct, etc.) and programme them into your phone and/ or write them on a pad near your landline phone.

Assign specific areas for your BT and their equipment

You need to make room for your new BT:

- Assign a place in your room for your BT to sleep in. The Foundation for the Study of Infant Deaths (FSID) recommends that BTs sleep in their parents' room for the first six months. See *Chapter 2: New Recruits: Surviving the First 24 Hours* for more information on how to prepare a bed. Ensure you have made your base camp safe and baby proof. In addition:

- ○ Block draughts from windows and doors. It is important to maintain a constant temperature in the room where your BT sleeps. Use your room thermometer to keep the temperature between 16 and 20°C (61–68°F). The ideal is 18°C (64°F).
  - ○ Do not put the cot directly next to a heater, a radiator or in direct sunlight.
- Assign a nappy-changing station. This will include all you need to change your BT, from water and cotton wool to nappy bags. I preferred to make mine portable, because my BT was. Ideally, you need to see all the contents so you know when and what to replenish. Replenish often. I used a small bathroom storage rack with wheels for my mobile changing station.
- Assign a feeding station: in the room where your wife or partner is most comfortable, create a feeding station. It can be as simple as a comfortable chair, a supportive U-shaped cushion, somewhere safe to put a drink, etc. It should include all the equipment she will need for breastfeeding. If she is comfortable breastfeeding in different rooms, make this a portable station.
- Assign suitable places in your base camp to keep bulky but essential items, from bags of nappies to car seats and buggies.

Essentials you need when bringing your BT from hospital to base camp

Clothes

Soft, breathable and accessible clothes. This means cotton with no frills or buttons. Keep their hands and feet covered, as their extremities get cold easily. As a general rule, BTs require one more layer than adults do, unless the weather is very hot.

- A babygro, a sleepsuit, a hat, socks and scratch mittens.
- If the weather is cold, pack a baby blanket (sometimes called a receiving blanket) or two.
- If very cold, take a snowsuit, but you must be able to strap your BT into their car seat correctly and without causing discomfort.

Changing
- A 'top and tail' kit comprising a small container for fresh water and cotton wool balls for cleaning purposes. It is not recommended to use wipes for your BT's first six months.
- Nappies.

Transport
A car seat that conforms to safety standards. See *Chapter 10: On Manoeuvres: Transporting the Troops* for guidance on car seat safety.

COMMANDO DAD TERMS USED IN THIS CHAPTER

Base camp: home.

Bomb disposal: emptying dirty nappies into outside bins every night.

BT: baby trooper. A trooper (child) before it is mobile.

Cookhouse: kitchen.

Recce: short for reconnaissance, a mission to obtain information. In this context, to understand the situation.

SOP: standard operating procedure. Something that must always be done in the same way.

Up to speed: where all relevant information, and the mission and actions to carry out, are clear.

CHAPTER 2:
NEW RECRUITS:
SURVIVING THE FIRST
24 HOURS

The brief:
Basic does not always mean simple. Commando Dad basics are the key skills that you need to master in order to be an effective carer for your BT.

Objective:
By the end of today's briefing you will have a greater understanding of the skills you need to survive the first 24 hours, and the weeks beyond, when you have a BT in your base camp:

- How to hold your BT.
- How to change a disposable nappy.
- How to clean a stump.
- Bottle administration.
  - How to sterilise trooper bottles and make, heat and cool bottles of formula or breast milk.
- How to bottle-feed your BT.
- How to burp your BT.
- How to prepare a bed for your BT.
- Beyond the first 24 hours.
  - How to bath your BT.
  - How to take your BT out and about.
- How to deal with crying.
- Survive the first 24 hours.

How to hold your BT

- When picking up your BT, slide your hands under their head and bottom, and lift their whole body.
- If your BT is handed to you, put one hand under their head and one under their body.
- When sitting with your BT, rest their head in the crook of your arm, or hold them against your shoulder, with one hand supporting the head and neck and the other under their bottom.

Do:

- Always support your BT's head (they won't be able to support their own head for at least the first month).
- Move slowly.

Don't:

- Pick up or put down your BT roughly.

For a video showing how to pick up and hold your BT correctly, go to *Resources* on www.commandodad.com.

How to change a disposable nappy

The golden rules of nappy changing:

- Change the nappy as soon as you can after it has been filled. It will protect your BT from discomfort and nappy rash.
- Make the nappy-changing process as quick as possible. It will protect you from negligent discharge.
- **Wipe boy BTs** around the testicles and penis, but don't pull back the foreskin.
- **Wipe girl BTs** from front to back to avoid infection.
- **Never** leave your BT unattended during the changing process.

You will need:

- A stable surface.
- A changing mat (if you're out and about take a portable changing mat or a clean towel). A clean changing mat turns a number of suitable surfaces (floor, sofa, bed, etc.) into suitable changing areas.
- Clean nappies.
- Clean hands.
- Bag to put the dirty nappy in, if required.
- A clean cloth, or cotton wool with tepid water. It is not recommended that wipes be used on BTs under the age of six months.

Within a short period of time you will be able to do this with your eyes shut, which will become essential for nocturnal missions (when you want to feed and change your BT without switching all the lights on). For now, keep your eyes open.

1. Get everything you need, wash your hands and open the nappy.

2. Lay your BT on a clean, comfortable, stable surface.

3. With one hand resting gently on your BT's stomach, use the other hand to undo the two plastic tabs and open the front of the used nappy.

4. Using the hand that was resting on your BT's stomach, gently lift your BT by the ankles, just enough to lift their bottom off the mat and wipe them from front to back with their nappy, close the nappy and then lower your BT back on to it. Having your BT rest their bottom on the used nappy saves your clean mat.

5. Using the wipes or water, clean your BT thoroughly. Check that your BT's fat folds and back are clean. While your BT has a stump, you will need to keep it clean and dry. See below for a useful method.

6. Lift your BT once more, remove the dirty nappy and slide the clean, open one underneath.

7. The tabs (on the back of the nappy) should be in line with your BT's belly button. Fasten the nappy but not too tightly. Elasticated legs prevent leakages, not tight waistbands. Nappies should leave no marks. If they do, they are too tight, or too small. Fold the waistband down while your BT still has a stump.

8. Prepare the dirty nappy for disposal. Put the dirty wipes or cotton balls inside, fold it up as tightly as possible, and fasten it with its own tabs. You may wish to use a bag to put the nappy in, especially if it's an explosive bowel movement, or howitzer. Even if using nappy bags, empty your indoor bin daily – bomb disposal.

9. Dress your BT.

10. Wash your hands.

Occasionally a BT will fire a howitzer into their nappy, and in those cases, nothing stops it. BTs can literally be up to their necks in it.

For step-by-step videos on how to change disposable and non-disposable nappies, see *Resources* on www.commandodad.com. You will also find information there on other washable nappy products available on the market.

COMMANDO DAD TOP TIP

If you are using a mobile changing station like I did, get into the habit of changing your BT in places where they can't easily roll off – i.e. in the middle of a bed or on the floor. Do this right from the beginning and then you will not get caught out when they learn to roll.

How to clean a stump (umbilical cord)

clean hands

comfortable and stable surface

clean stump with cotton wool

You will need:

- A stable surface.
- Clean hands.
- Cotton wool, clean luke warm water.

Your BT is issued with a stump (what is left of the umbilical cord). It will drop off naturally a week or so after birth and reveal a belly button. You must keep the stump dry and clean (to prevent infection) until that time. You will need to clean the stump every time you change your BT's nappy.

There are numerous methods for this. Here's the method I used with my three BTs:

- Be very gentle. Do not pull the stump. The skin underneath (what will become the belly button) must heal naturally or your BT may get an infection.
- Keep the stump dry. Do not immerse your BT in a bath until the stump has fallen off. Instead, give your baby a sponge bath.
- Fold the waistband of your BT's nappy down so that it doesn't cover or rub the stump.

It is normal for:

- The stump to turn black and wizened, like a frostbitten fingertip.
- The stump to be sticky at the base.
- The wound to take a week or so to heal after the stump falls off.
- The stump to smell.

It is not normal for:

- The stump to weep.
- The stump or abdomen to become red and swollen.

If you have any concerns about your BT's stump, seek advice from your medical support team: health visitor, doctor, nurse or pharmacist.

Bottle administration

How to sterilise a trooper's bottle

You will need to sterilise your BT's bottles, and dummies, for at least their first year as their immune systems are still developing.

You will need:

- Clean hands.
- Detergent (normal washing-up liquid, for example).
- Bottlebrush (only used for this purpose).
- Your sterilising equipment of choice:
  - A saucepan (used only for this purpose) and water.
  - An electric or microwave steam steriliser.
  - A cold-water sterilisation solution.

It is impossible to live in a germ-free environment, but you can make your BT ill if you do not scrupulously clean bottles and dummies. Do not put the – avoidable – stress of an ill BT upon the unit. Here are the golden rules of sterilising:

1. Wash hands.
2. Using hot water, detergent and a bottlebrush, thoroughly clean the bottle, cap and teat (and ring if your bottle has it). Turn the teat inside out and scrub the inside. Rinse the bottle, cap and teat.
3. Discard cracked bottles.
4. Sterilise. You can do any of the following:
    - Boil all parts of the bottle for ten minutes in a saucepan (but this can wear out teats quickly).
    - Use an electric or microwave steam steriliser. Usually takes a few minutes and the bottles can be stored in the steriliser, keeping them sterile for hours (check manufacturer's instructions).
    - Use a cold-water sterilisation solution. This allows you to soak bottles for up to 24 hours. You will need to buy sterilisation tablets regularly.
5. Wash hands before touching sterile items. Keep bottles sterile until needed by either leaving them in the steriliser or storing them in the fridge.

Dishwashers are only suitable for washing bottles – not for sterilising, as they are not hot enough. Water needs to be boiling to make bottles sterile.

For a video showing how to sterilise a bottle, go to *Resources* on www.commandodad.com.

How to make a bottle of breast milk

If your partner expresses breast milk, she will need clean hands and a clean, sterilised container to put the breast milk in. If she is using a breast pump, ensure that the pump is clean and sterilised before every use. If you plan to use the breast milk within the next few hours or days – breast milk can be stored in the fridge for up to three days at 4°C – then, ideally, express into a sterilised bottle. If using another sterilised container, ensure that you put it into clean, sterilised bottles before giving it to your BT.

Milk stored in the fridge may separate. This is normal. Just shake gently.

Breast milk can be frozen and kept for up to three months in the freezer. It can be frozen in sterilised bottles or special plastic breast-milk bags, but don't fill the milk up to the very top as milk expands during freezing. Frozen breast milk will need to be defrosted in the fridge before being given to your BT. Breast milk cannot be refrozen.

How to make a bottle of formula milk

Ideally, make bottles as you need them. Mix formula into cold water and bring to body temperature, either by immersing bottle into warm water, or use a bottle warmer.

You will need:

- A tin of powdered formula, suitable for newborns.
- A sterilised bottle.
- Clean, steady hands.

Every tin of formula has clear instructions on the side from the manufacturer. Follow them exactly, every time. This is non-negotiable. Never guess amounts, because too much or too little formula will cause real problems. Too little may not provide your BT with enough nourishment, and too much may cause constipation and dehydration.

Use the following advice to make formula feeding as safe as possible:

1. Pour water in the bottle. Take care to get amounts exact. Add cold water to required amount of formula.
2. Using the scoop provided, measure out the formula. After scooping, gently tap the side of the scoop with a clean knife to make sure there are no air pockets (do not pack the powder down), level off the scoop with the back of the knife.
3. Assemble the bottle, including the cover, and shake well until all the powder has dissolved. If you can't find the cover, use the tip of your (very clean) finger to cover the hole in the teat before shaking.
4. Warm the bottle as described above.

Take care to make the appropriate volume of formula for your BT's age, as the remains of a bottle of formula milk must be discarded (because bacteria will grow in the remains).

How much milk will your BT need?
Unhelpfully, there is no one answer. As you get more used to your BT, you will be able to decipher both their 'I'm hungry' and 'I'm full' cues, and then you can let them set the pace. Until that point it can be helpful to have a *minimum* amount as a rough guide. To get that amount, multiply your BT's weight in pounds by two and this is the least amount of milk, in ounces, that they need to take in over a 24-hour period.

For a video showing how to make a bottle of formula,
go to *Resources* on www.commandodad.com

How to heat a bottle of formula or breast milk

1. As already mentioned, BT's milk should be given to them at body temperature and no warmer.

2. Do not heat milk in a microwave as it heats unevenly, and quickly. Too much heat is bad for breast milk and can also cause pockets of very hot milk, which can burn your BT.

3. Heat gently. Put the bottle of milk in a bowl or pan of hot (but not boiling) water.

4. Take the bottle out and swirl the contents to ensure even distribution of heat.

5. Do the wrist test to check temperature.

6. Always err on the side of caution. Repeat steps 4 and 5 until you are confident that the bottle is cool enough.

If you are out and about, try and secure access to a cookhouse to warm bottles. If this is not possible, consider buying an insulated bottle carrier. This will enable you to warm bottles at base camp, and keep them warm until needed. Breast milk can be warmed to body temperature by placing in a pocket, under the arm, etc. or allowed to warm at room temperature. But any breast milk left after an hour should be discarded.

For a video showing how to heat milk, go to
Resources on www.commandodad.com.

How to bottle-feed your BT

You will need:

- Clean hands.
- A clean bottle, loaded with fresh formula or breast milk.
- A comfortable place to sit so that you don't need to keep changing position and disturbing your BT.

A successful feed is one in which your BT swallows milk, not air. So:

1. Keep your BT propped up in your arms when feeding, so that they can breathe and swallow. Always support your BT's head as they will not be able to support their own heads until they are at least six months old.
2. Tilt the bottle so that the teat is full of milk, not air.
3. Place the teat against the top of your BT's mouth.
4. Sometimes your BT may suck so hard the teat on the bottle flattens and the milk stops flowing. In this case, very gently twist the bottle to release the vacuum.
5. Let your BT have a rest during a feed if they want one. In these instances, burp them gently.
6. When your BT has finished their feed, burp them gently.
7. Discard unused formula feed and refrigerate unused expressed breast milk in a sterilised bottle, with a sterilised teat.

For a video showing how to feed a BT, go to *Resources* on www.commandodad.com.

How to burp your BT

Trapped wind can be very painful. Don't let your BT suffer. Make burping a key element of your feeding routine. Every time. Gentle burping will reduce stomach bloating and will prevent your BT throwing up, even if it may not seem like it at the time.

You will need:

- A burp cloth: literally any soft, clean cloth that you can drape over your shoulder to make your BT comfortable and catch any regurgitated milk.

Always:

- Support your BT's head.
- Be patient. Burps may not come straight away, if at all.

There are several different ways to burp a BT. This is the most common:

- Put your burp cloth over your shoulder.
- Lay your BT so that their head rests on your shoulder and their stomach is against your chest.
- Alternate between gently patting your BT's back and rubbing in a circular motion until they burp (and sometimes they may not).
- Walking around may help soothe your BT if trapped wind is making them uncomfortable.

Other methods of burping

- Sit your BT upright on your lap. Provide support by resting your hand against your BT's chest and rest their chin between your thumb and index finger. Use the other hand to rub your BT's back as above.
- Lay your BT on their belly in your lap. Support their head and make sure it's higher than their chest. Use the other hand to rub your baby's back as above.

For videos of these methods for burping BTs, go to
Resources on www.commandodad.com.

How to prepare a bed for your BT

After the first six weeks you can start getting your BT into a sleep routine. See *Chapter 3: Sleep and Other Nocturnal Missions* for what to do at that stage. Until then:

- Keep babies close, in your room. This is comforting for your BT and may make it easier for you and your partner – especially if she is breastfeeding.
- Do not have your BT sleep in your bed, especially at this young age. It is too easy for you or your partner to roll onto them during the night. It is simply not worth the risk.
- If you are using a cot straight away, assemble it in your room. Use a Moses basket within the cot for the first few months. BTs risk getting too cold in a large bed. Using a Moses basket will make it easier to bring your BT's bed with you wherever you go.
- In either case ensure your BT is as safe as possible by following the advice given by the Foundation for the Study of Infant Deaths (FSID):
  - There must be no pillows or quilts in the cot or Moses basket. Cover your BT with thin layers of breathable fabric or use a baby sleeping bag.

grip tape strips on
hood and liner pressed
firmly together

sheet and mattress
on bottom of
basket

liner hugs the rim
around all sides

tabs wrapped and secured
around handles on both
sides

- The mattress must fit snugly to prevent your BT getting trapped between the mattress and the cot. It must be waterproof to ensure it can be kept thoroughly clean and dry.

- Your BT must always lie on their back with their feet touching the bottom of the cot or Moses basket to prevent them wriggling down under the covers.

- Leave your BT's head uncovered to prevent overheating.

- Room temperature is important. The ideal temperature is 18°C (64°F), and you can either use your central-heating thermostat or buy a room thermometer to ensure optimum temperature.

Beyond the first 24 hours:

How to bath your BT

Babies do not need to be washed daily and bathing is not recommended for at least the first week to allow the Vernix (nature's moisturiser, the white coating covering your BT at birth) to sink in effectively.

You will need to wash your BT's hands, face, neck and genitals every day.

You only need to bath your BT two to three times a week.

You may choose to do it more often, but not less. Hair will only need washing once a week.

I used a baby bath while my BTs were small, but a clean kitchen sink is an ideal place to bathe your BT.

Follow these safety tips for bathing the BT:

Do:

- Support your BT. Lower them gently into the bath using one hand to hold their upper arm and support their head and shoulders making sure the BT's body is fully immersed – exposed skin can cool quickly and make your BT cold. Get a firm hold as BTs can become slippery when wet. Use your other hand to gently wash water over your BT's body.

- Wash your BT's face gently with a clean, wet washcloth before bathing. You don't need to use soap or baby wash, just water. Take care to keep your BT's head out of the bath water.

- Pour cold water in the bath first, then hot. Water needs to be warm. You can ensure the right temperature (about 37°C) by using a thermometer or your elbow.

- Make the bath water deep enough to cover trunk and limbs of BT.

- Use pH-neutral shampoo and baby wash, as it will not irritate your BT's skin or sting if it gets into their eyes. Babies can splash soapy water into their eyes with startling accuracy.

- Be gentle. Wash BTs with a soft flannel.

Don't:

- Forget to check your BT's nappy before bathtime. If your BT's had a poo, clean them as you normally would, before putting them in the bath.

- Leave your BT unattended for any reason. Don't even turn your back to them. Ignore interruptions. If you need to tend to something, wrap them up and take them with you.

- Put your BT in the water while the taps are running.

- Give your BT their first few baths at night. It is a mistake to introduce new things close to bedtime as it could stimulate your BT.

- Bath your BT in a cold room.

Make it an SOP (standard operating procedure) to dry BT thoroughly, wrap warmly and cuddle for at least ten minutes after being in a bath. Your BT gets cold easily and needs your body heat to get warmed up again.

For a video on how to bath your BT, go to *Resources* on www.commandodad.com.

How to take your BT out and about

There is no medical reason why you shouldn't take healthy newborn BTs out and about. It will be great for you to get out in the fresh air and also to meet other parents (see *Chapter 7: Morale: A Commando Dad's Secret Weapon* for more details about the importance of a support network.)

However, very young BTs do not have strong immune systems and crowds (supermarkets, Tube stations, etc.) should ideally be avoided, or at least limited. In the very early days (i.e. the first few weeks), before you are familiar with how to feed and change your BT, I would not advise yomping. Stay near to base camp, and therefore all supplies. Beyond that, just make sure you have your basic survival kit squared away before leaving base camp.

Dress your BT appropriately for the weather and the transport needed. If the weather is cool, use warm, breathable clothes and a hat; if the weather is hot, use sunscreen and a sun hat or shade.

COMMANDO DAD TOP TIP

I used a baby carrier (not a sling) to transport my BTs. It enabled me to hold them close to my body but left my hands free for my many other tasks. I always made sure that my BT didn't get too hot by dressing them in light layers. Definitely no thick woollen layers. See *Chapter 10: On Manoeuvres: Transporting the Troops* for information on carriers and other options for moving around with your troopers.

How to deal with crying

In the early days, your BT will communicate with you in the only way available to them: by crying. You may not believe this now, but within weeks you will start to recognise their different cries. Until then, use this useful checklist:

- **Hunger**: Babies process food quickly. Hence the multiple nappies. Offer them a feed.
- **Discomfort**: Check the nappy. Dirty, wet nappies are a clear source of discomfort. Check clothes aren't too tight anywhere on the body, or that anything is causing them discomfort. Check the environment, e.g. for temperature, noise, breeze, lumps in the mattress. Burp them. Make sure they're not too hot or too cold.
- **Tiredness**: Babies need a lot of sleep. They went through labour and now are processing a huge amount of information from a stimulating world. Give them plenty of opportunities to sleep it off.
- **Illness**: Look for symptoms: a temperature, sickness, diarrhoea, a rash. Act. Seek advice from your medical support team: midwife, health visitor, doctor, nurse or pharmacist. In the early days, before you have learned to recognise the symptoms of trooper ailments, let the professionals make that call. Do not be concerned about troubling your medical team with 'minor' concerns. You will find more details about common BT ailments in *Chapter 8: Call the Medic: Basic First Aid and Unit Maintenance*.

COMMANDO DAD TOP TIP

Buy a set of earplugs. Don't sleep in them but wear them when dealing with your crying BT. To a new Commando Dad, a lot of crying can be stressful. Reduce the volume and pitch by wearing earplugs. You will be amazed what a difference it makes.

COMMANDO DAD TERMS USED IN THIS CHAPTER

Base camp: home.

Bomb disposal: emptying dirty nappies into outside bins every night.

BT: baby trooper. A trooper (child) before it is mobile.

Cookhouse: kitchen.

Howitzer: the explosive contents of a nappy.

Negligent discharge: when you accidentally fire a round when you weren't meant to. In this instance, used to describe the ability of a BT to pee or poop the moment their nappy is removed.

SOP: standard operating procedure. Something that must always be done in the same way.

Unit: family.

Yomping: a long, active walk.

CHAPTER 3:
SLEEP AND OTHER NOCTURNAL MISSIONS

The brief:
Sleep deprivation is tough. For the sake of the health and well-being of the unit, you need to ensure that you all get as much sleep as possible and that you introduce an effective sleep routine.

Objective:
Today's briefing is an introduction to sleep routines. Recce the Internet and bookshops, and speak to your health visitor for information to supplement what you will learn today. You will find extra information under *Resources* on www.commandodad.com.

By the end of today's briefing you will have a greater understanding of:
- Sleep routine: what it is and how, and when, to introduce it.
    - Golden rules.
    - Techniques for establishing a sleep routine.
- What to do when your BT wakes at night.
- Nap routine.
    - Common nap cues.
- Sleep deprivation.
    - How to get help.

Sleep routine: what it is and how, and when, to introduce it

Getting your BT into a sleep routine is very important. <u>But do not attempt to introduce a sleep routine for the first six to eight weeks.</u> In this period your BT is unable to stay awake for more than a few hours during a 24-hour period.

They need to:

- Learn the difference between night and day.
- Reset their body clock: during pregnancy the physical activity of your partner during the day would rock them into submission but in the evening, when she went to bed, the rocking would stop and your BT would become more physically active. Therefore your BT arrived with a body clock that is the exact opposite of what you need it to be.

After eight weeks you need to introduce a sleep routine. This may prove difficult but the rewards are worth it. You and your partner will be able to get more R&R, and your BT will learn how to go to sleep and settle at night. This will pay dividends for years to come.

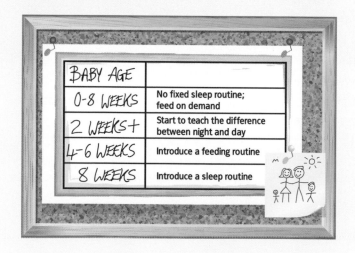

BABY AGE	
0-8 WEEKS	No fixed sleep routine; feed on demand
2 WEEKS+	Start to teach the difference between night and day
4-6 WEEKS	Introduce a feeding routine
8 WEEKS	Introduce a sleep routine

Golden rules for introducing a sleep routine

The foundation of a sleep routine is to introduce predictability: activities that happen at the same time every day. One of those activities will soon become your BT's sleep routine.

Teach your BT the difference between night and day

Do:

- Make daytime more active.
- Make sure the house is bright during the day.
- Make night-time quieter and more subdued.

Don't:

- Tiptoe round your BT or operate silent running during daytime naps. BTs need to be exposed to the regular sounds of a house during the day: the phone, talking, laughing, the radio, TV, loo flushing, etc.
- After the first 6–8 weeks, don't let your BT continue to nap if it is time for a feed. Wake them up gently.
- Use the 'big light' at night. Dim the lights or use lamps.

Introduce an evening routine

After a stimulating day and a calm evening, get your BT ready for bed. Remember that a sleep routine is not appropriate for BTs under six weeks.

- Ensure your BT is clean and comfortable and has a clean nappy.
- Offer the last feed of the day to your BT.

For details of useful routines for older MTs, see the 'Lights out: evening routine' section of *Chapter 6: Standing Orders: Establishing Daily Routines.*

Techniques for establishing a sleep routine

There are many different techniques for getting your BT off to sleep. I have detailed the method that worked successfully for me below. If you like the sound of it, try it. If you don't like the sound of it, don't try it. There is no guaranteed, single method of getting a BT to sleep. You need to find one that you are comfortable with.

1. Put your BT down in their cot or Moses basket when they are tired, but still awake. Learning to drop off alone is an important step to an undisturbed night's sleep, for both of you.
2. Ensure they are comfortable, kiss them and leave the room.
3. If your BT starts to cry, and they probably will, be prepared to let them cry, initially for a maximum of five minutes.
4. If they are still crying after five minutes, go into the room and check them. Gently make sure they are not wet, or uncomfortable. They should not be hungry if they recently had a feed. Operate silent running. If you get angry or frustrated you will upset your BT.
5. Repeat steps 2–4, gradually increase the time they are left to cry until they fall asleep over a period of days.
6. Never leave your BT to cry for more than 20 minutes.

It is normal for:

- Your BT to have trouble settling and to cry.
- Your BT to take a long time to go to sleep – they are learning a completely new skill.
- Your BT to fall out of their routine (it's common for a BT to wake up during the night again after they have begun to sleep through).

It is not normal for:

- Your BT to have a temperature or a rash. If in doubt, seek medical help.
- Your BT to have intense, unexplained fussing (discontentment and

crying) and/or screaming that lasts for hours, especially after a feed or in the evening. In this case your BT may have colic. Be prepared for intense periods of soothing your BT: rocking, burping, massage, etc. See *Chapter 8: Call the Medic: Basic First Aid and Unit Maintenance* for more information on colic and other illnesses.

COMMANDO DAD TOP TIP

The first time I let my BT cry for 20 minutes it seemed like the longest 20 minutes of my life. But a cry is the only way your BT can communicate with you. They are not necessarily crying out of distress. They could be complaining that they weren't ready for bed, that they just want your attention, or that life isn't fair. Later on, when your MTs can verbalise these complaints, you will remember this non-vocal period fondly.

What to do when your BT wakes at night

When tending to your BT during the night, remember <u>it is not a social event</u>.

Do:

- Operate silent running and keep talking to an absolute minimum.
- Be gentle, calm and quiet.
- Be quick and efficient so that your BT – and you – can be back in bed as soon as possible.

Don't:

- Use the 'big light'.
- Stimulate your BT.

Your BT is most likely waking for a feed but also take the opportunity to check:

- Your BT's nappy. If it is dirty, change it. If the cot sheet is wet, change that too.
- If your BT is comfortable.
- Your BT's environment: were they woken by a noise? A light?

It takes 30 minutes for your eyes to properly adjust to the dark and for you to acquire night vision, so ideally have a night light or lamp with a low-wattage bulb in the same room as your BT. Don't put on the 'big light' as it will startle and stimulate your BT.

COMMANDO DAD TOP TIP

You may need to tend to your BT several times throughout the night. Until your BT can sleep for several hours in one go, you need to master the art of the power nap: grabbing sleep when and where you can, day or night. If you are not engaged in looking after your BT or other troopers in your unit, your number one priority should be to get some sleep. You will feel better and more able to cope with the rigours of parenting.

Nap routine

Once you have established your sleep routine, BTs (and MTs) will still need to nap during the day.

Do:

- Choose your sleep battles wisely and respect your BT's natural sleep patterns as much as you can. They will naturally want to sleep at certain times of the day. Do not let them sleep too long, however. Babies over 6–8 weeks will need to be gently woken from a nap if it is time for a feed.

- Arrange daytime activities around your BT's nap (e.g. you don't want to plan a play date right before nap time).

Don't:

- Let your BT nap too late in the evening, as this will affect a good night's sleep.

The nap routine should mirror the night-time routine (without the calming down beforehand). You will need to:

- Make sure your BT is not hungry.
- Make sure your BT has a clean nappy.
- Lay your BT down tired, but not asleep.

COMMANDO DAD TOP TIP

If your BT falls asleep when you are out on a sortie (when they are in a car seat or pushchair), always take them out of their transport and lay them flat in their bed when you get to base camp. It is not healthy for a BT to spend too much time in a car seat or pushchair. Being in a semi-upright position for long periods may place a strain on their developing spine.

Common nap cues

Some babies will need a lot of daytime sleep, and some won't. Learn to decipher your BT's sleep cues.

- Yawning and/or rubbing eyes.
- Losing interest in activities, and in you or other adults.

- Getting restless and fidgeting.
- Crying (a late signal).

> # COMMANDO DAD TOP TIP
> You may notice that some common sleep cues are the same as common hunger cues. This is because your BT has limited methods at their disposal to communicate with you. Weigh up all other factors to decide what your BT is trying to tell you.

Sleep deprivation

Do not underestimate the negative effect of sleep deprivation. If you find that sleep deprivation is making you or your partner irritable, frustrated or angry, act now.

- Share your experiences with other parents. We all have our battle stories and it will make you feel less isolated.
- If you are unable to share childcare equally with your partner, ask a relative to watch your BT so you can get some sleep.
- If you are alone with your BT and feel stressed and angry, put them down somewhere safe – such as their cot – and take ten minutes to calm down.
- Break state. Splash your face with cold water, breathe calmly, play some of your favourite music.
- Keep your morale high. See *Chapter 7: Morale: A Commando Dad's Secret Weapon* for advice and guidance.

Where to get help

If you continue to feel angry, or find yourself getting angry quickly and often, tell a close friend, your health visitor or doctor. If you do not feel able to reach out in this way, and would prefer to remain anonymous, call the Samaritans or reach out to other parents in online chat rooms.

This does not make you a failure as a parent. It shows great strength of character to recognise that you need help and even greater strength of character to act on it. Do not delay.

COMMANDO DAD TERMS USED IN THIS CHAPTER

Base camp: home.
BT: baby trooper. A trooper (child) before it is mobile.
MT: mobile trooper. A trooper that can shuffle, crawl, stand up and, eventually, walk.
Silent running: continuing to operate normally, but in silence or near silence (as used on submarines).

CHAPTER 4:
KITBAGS: PACKING EVERYDAY ESSENTIALS

The brief:

A kitbag contains the essentials you need in any situation; no more, no less. It is too easy to over-pack or under-pack kitbags. These are potentially hazardous situations to be avoided at all costs.

Objective:

By the end of today's briefing you will know how to pack the following:

- Basic survival kit.
- Basic survival kit for light-order missions: essential items for short sorties away from base camp.
- Basic survival kit for mid-term deployment: essential items for extended times away from base camp, such as long car or train journeys, or flights.
- Basic survival kit for long-term major deployment (holidays).
- Packing a kitbag: packing clothes for long-term major deployment (holidays).
  - Golden rules and tips for packing clothes.

Basic survival kit

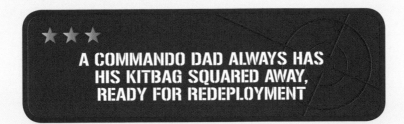

★ ★ ★

A COMMANDO DAD ALWAYS HAS HIS KITBAG SQUARED AWAY, READY FOR REDEPLOYMENT

To follow is your essential kit list for a BT and MT. Make it an SOP to check your basic survival kit at the start of every day. Do not attempt to leave the house without it. Your sanity will, at some point, depend on it.

- Wipes.
- Nappies.
- Small pot of nappy-rash cream (which also acts as a sunblock, and a cream for cuts, grazes and sunburn).
- Clean dummy (if used) with cover.
- Clean plastic spoon in a plastic bag.
- Bibs.
- One complete change of clothes.
- Antibacterial hand gel.
- Nappy bags or plastic bags.
- Portable changing mat (or a clean towel will suffice).
- Flannel.
- Basic First Aid Kit. See *Chapter 8: Call the Medic: Basic First Aid and Unit Maintenance* for appropriate contents.
- Spare keys to your house/car.

Keep this kit in a dedicated bag. This will make it easy to find, easy to replenish and easy to keep squared away. Ideally, use a rucksack as this will allow you to keep both hands free when on the move.

Basic survival kit for light-order missions

Depending on the length of your trip away from base camp – or sortie – the basic survival kit will normally suffice, although you may wish to add snacks. See *Chapter 5: Nutrition: An Army Marches on its Stomach* for some good options.

COMMANDO DAD TOP TIP

All contents of your basic survival kit are non-perishable. This is intentional. Clear it out often, as it will inevitably become the home for perishable items. I put the contents of my basic survival kit in a plastic bag before putting it in my rucksack. This not only protects against inclement weather and spillages, but also makes the bag easier to clear out. The natural law of crumb attraction states that this bag, and any kind of troop transportation – from cars to buggies – will become a powerful magnet for all food detritus.

If you are out and about, and your BT/MT has an explosive incident involving a bodily function, change them immediately. Rinse clothes if possible, before putting them in a nappy sack or plastic bag. This will protect your basic survival kit, and your noses, until you can get back to base camp. If you have no access to washing facilities, wash them down the best you can with a flannel and bottled water, or wipes. If your BT/MT is uncomfortable, plan an immediate return to base.

Basic survival kit for mid-term deployment

When you are going to be away from base for an extended amount of time with your BT/MT – but not overnight – you need the following essential kit.

1. Basic survival kit for light-order missions, plus:
2. Rations: ensure you have enough food and drink for the time spent away from base camp.

3. A small flask of hot water to make bottles/reconstitute dried baby food (if your journey covers a mealtime and you will be in transit at that point).

Ideally, make bottles as you need them. Only make formula in advance if you know you will not have access to a clean cookhouse and a kettle for the next feed(s). Store bottles and formula in the fridge for up to twelve hours and in a cool bag for no more than four. Be aware you will need to heat the milk, which can be as time-consuming as making fresh bottles. As an alternative, you can store unused hot water in a flask and use this to make future feeds on the move.

When in transit with your troopers you will also need to include at least one activity/toy in your kit. See *Chapter 11: Entertaining the Troops* for engaging activities.

Basic survival kit for long-term deployment (holidays)

When you are staying away from base overnight, or for any number of nights, with your BT/MT, you will need the following essential kit:

1. Basic survival kit for light-order missions, plus:
2. Appropriate clothes for the trip (see 'Packing a kitbag', below, for tips).
3. Bottles and cleaning equipment. Secure access to the cookhouse to clean bottles properly.
4. The trigger your BT/MT uses to go to sleep every night (teddy, blanket, dummy, etc.)
5. Night-time nappies (if used).

If you are taking your BT/MT to stay in a place without a cot (always check ahead), take a travel cot or carrycot. These can be heavy and bulky, so try to ensure access to a cot at your destination. A good alternative is a baby bed designed for camping, which is lightweight and can double up as a sunshade.

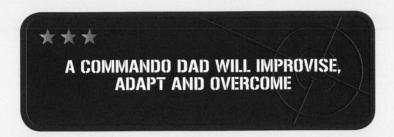

★ ★ ★

A COMMANDO DAD WILL IMPROVISE, ADAPT AND OVERCOME

For all types of deployments you will need to factor in transport. See *Chapter 10: On Manoeuvres: Transporting the Troops* for advice.

Packing a kitbag: packing clothes for long-term deployment (holidays)

Don't over-pack clothes – for yourself or your troopers. This results in lugging around kitbags of unworn clothes. Not a smart move.

The golden rules for packing a kitbag are:

- Pack for the weather/activities you will be undertaking.
- Pack for the days you will be away and count travel clothes as one day.
- Don't pack a separate set of clothes for every eventuality. Pack versatile clothes that can be used in a number of situations.

There follows a sample packing list for a week away with a BT/MT (girl or boy). The weather is typically British; a bit cold; a bit windy; a bit warm; a bit wet.

- Underwear and sock pairs x 6 (they are wearing one set).
- Bottoms x 4 (jeans, sweats, dungarees, shorts, etc. all constitute 'bottoms').
- Waterproof coat (ideally have them travel in this).
- Tops x 5 (long-sleeved T-shirts, short-sleeved T-shirts, shirts, etc. all constitute tops).
- Thin jumper/fleece x 2 (layering with thin clothes is much more effective

at keeping your troopers (and you) warm than using thick jumpers and fleeces. It also gives you all an opportunity to vent; if you start to get hot you can remove a layer or two and still be warm.

- Shoes x 3 pairs (wellingtons, trainers, sandals, shoes, etc. all constitute shoes).
- Hat.
- Sunglasses if appropriate.
- Sleepwear x 2.
- Swimwear x 1.
- Toothbrush and toothpaste.

If you can secure access to washing facilities it will be possible to reduce the items on the packing list.

COMMANDO DAD TOP TIP

I have not included dresses or skirts for girls because, when packing for my daughter, I have never found them to be as versatile as tops and bottoms. You may disagree. In which case categorise a dress as a 'top'.

Exceptions

- Babies: very young babies will always get through an incredible amount of bibs, babygros and sleepsuits as they get to grips with controlling their bodily functions. Always ration for twice as many as the days you will be away and secure access to washing facilities.
- Underwear and socks: always have a set of underwear and socks for every day, regardless of access to washing facilities. Trust me on this one.

Tips for packing

- Roll your clothes as it saves space and creases.
- Wear the bulkiest items for the journey.
- Fill spaces, e.g. shoes or the edges of your bag, with smaller items such as socks and underwear.
- Pack the items you'll need first – e.g. swimsuit or pyjamas – last, so they are at the top of your case.
- Pack a plastic bag to keep dirty clothes in.

Snacks

For ideas on ideal snacks for life on the move, see 'Real food fast: snack packing' in *Chapter 5: Nutrition: An Army Marches on its Stomach*.

COMMANDO DAD TERMS USED IN THIS CHAPTER

Base camp: home.
BT: baby trooper. A trooper (child) before it is mobile.
Cookhouse: kitchen.
Light-order missions: short sorties away from base camp.
Long-term major deployment: holidays.
Mid-term deployment: extended times away from base camp, such as long car or train journeys, or flights.
MT: mobile trooper. A trooper that can shuffle, crawl, stand up and, eventually, walk.
Sortie: a trip away from base camp.
SOP: standard operating procedure. Something that must always be done in the same way.

CHAPTER 5:
NUTRITION: AN ARMY
MARCHES ON ITS STOMACH

The brief:
To be effective, your unit needs good food. Do not underestimate the benefits of a good diet, which include improved optimum growth and development, energy, better sleep, improved immunity to colds and other illnesses and a more positive outlook. It is never too early to start building good eating habits for your troopers, or too late to start improving your own.

Objective:
Today's briefing is an introduction to nutrition. Recce the Internet and bookshops, and speak to your health visitor for information to supplement what you will learn today. You will find extra information under *Resources* on www.commandodad.com.

- Weaning: what it is and how, and when, to deal with it.
  - Good first foods to experiment with and foods to avoid.
- Self-feeding: what it is and how, and when, to deal with it.
  - Good finger foods to experiment with.
- The importance of leading from the front and setting a good example.
- How to relieve the pain of teething.
- The golden rules of nutrition.
- The importance of portion sizes and a balanced diet.
- How to prepare nutritious foods for the unit.
  - Good ideas for breakfast, lunch and dinner.
  - How to introduce variety to prevent boredom.
- How to plan meals.
- How to prepare real food fast: healthy snacks.

For more information, books and resources that specialise in nutrition can be found in the *Nutrition* section, under *Resources*, on www.commandodad.com.

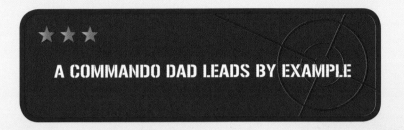

★ ★ ★

A COMMANDO DAD LEADS BY EXAMPLE

Weaning: what it is and how, and when, to deal with it

Weaning is when a BT moves from just milk to solid foods. This is where the 'fun' really starts. For a weaning BT, food is an interactive experience – allow them to taste it, touch it, look at it, smell it, wear it, throw it and, yes, even eat it.

Do:

- Stand your BT's high chair on a plastic, easy-clean surface (such as a wipe-clean tablecloth designed for camping).
- Have bibs and baby wipes to hand. A lot of them.
- Let your BT set the pace. Offer small amounts of food.
- Introduce new foods one at a time, and give them to your BT for two to three days. That way you will notice any adverse reactions and will be able to trace the trigger food. If you suspect that your child is suffering from a food allergy or intolerance, make an appointment with your GP.

Don't:

- Feed BTs when either of you are wearing clothes you would not happily see stained forever. The staining properties of BT's food are legendary. Do not underestimate them.

- Be tempted to continue to feed your BT in order to save the mess and to make feeding quicker. Weaning is an important part of your BT's development.
- Worry that your BT only wants to eat tiny amounts of food (or sometimes none at all). In the early days they will still be getting nutrition from their milk.
- Introduce protein or dairy products before six months – stick with the staples: baby rice, baby porridge, fruits and vegetables.

COMMANDO DAD TOP TIP

I always used absorbent bibs as I found that the food ran off wipe-clean bibs and on to my BT. I wanted my BT to stay clean rather than the bib. Just make sure you have plenty to hand as they'll get wet quickly. I found Velcro fastenings made it easier to get bibs on and off.

The World Health Organisation and the Department of Health recommend introducing solid food from six months. Look out for the following 'cues'. The British Dietetic Association (BDA) states the following applies to solid food introduction:

- Weaning should begin sometime around six months. Full-term BTs should begin weaning by six months but not earlier than 17 weeks.
- Pre-term BTs need special consideration and may benefit from delayed weaning – always speak to a health-care professional before beginning weaning a pre-term BT.
- Your BT can stay in a sitting position and hold their head steady.
- Your BT is very, very interested in watching you eat.
- Your BT is bringing their hands to their mouth and chewing down on things.

Good first foods to experiment with

- Baby cereal: rice or oat cereal, for example, made with breast or formula milk. A good way to introduce solids because it is a familiar, bland taste but a new texture.

- Puréed vegetables: carrot, butternut squash, courgette and parsnips are sweet-tasting, easy to cook and easy to purée. Start with root vegetables and progress to stronger tastes such as broccoli and cauliflower.

- Puréed fruit: start bland. Bananas, papaya, apples, pears and avocado. Use ripe fruit (look in supermarkets where ripe fruit is often sold very cheaply) as unripe fruit is simply too hard to mash. NB: if weaning before six months, your BT's milk intake should not decrease. Giving foods like banana and avocado can be very filling for small tummies and may result in a reduction of milk intake, so it's best to limit these foods in the early stages of weaning.

- Good-quality jars of baby food are readily available. Treat as you would any 'fresh' food once it has been opened. Limit use of shop-bought baby food to times when you are away from cooking facilities – try to stick to homemade foods as much as possible so that your BT gets used to home-cooked tastes.

COMMANDO DAD TOP TIP

There are certain types of food that cause allergic reactions more often than others. Don't introduce these foods – cow's milk, or any other dairy products, wheat and gluten, nuts, soya seeds, fish, shellfish and eggs – before six months.

Foods to avoid in the first year

- Excess/added salt – troopers between seven months and one year should have no more than 1 gram of salt per day, and troopers between one and three years old should have no more than 2 grams of salt per day. Salt can be found in many everyday items such as cereal, bread and cheese.
- Nuts.
- Nut butters (these are allowed if there is no history of allergies).
- Shellfish.
- Undercooked egg.
- Smoked/processed meat and fish.
- Refined sugar.
- Unpasteurised cheese/milk.
- Artificial sweeteners/colourings/flavouring and preservatives.
- Honey – May contain spores that are harmful to BTs under one year old.
- Hot and spicy food.

Self-feeding

This is when a BT begins to learn how to feed themselves with solid food. It starts with fingers – and finger food. Don't worry about KFS (cutlery).

Do:

- Feed your BT finger food in their high chair, laying the groundwork for eating at the table.
- Buy non-breakable plates. I found that learning to grab goes hand in hand with learning to throw.
- Continue to use protective equipment: bibs and a plastic sheet to stand the high chair on.

- Take extra special care – once your BT has the dexterity to pick up objects and put them in their mouth, they won't stop at food. They'll try and put everything in there.
- Do let your BT have their own spoon to practise with at mealtimes.

Don't:

- Leave your BT unsupervised when they are learning to self-feed.
- Feed finger foods in pushchairs or car seats. It is a choking risk for your BT.
- Give your BT 'hard' finger foods, or portions that are too large. Use your common sense and see suggestions below.
- Worry that your BT isn't using KFS (cutlery) to feed themselves. This ability comes several months after self-feeding begins.
- Offer finger foods that are refined, or high in sugar, fat or salt.

There is no golden rule for when to let your BT self-feed. Look out for the following 'cues' around six months and upwards:

- Your BT grabs your spoon when you are feeding them.
- Your BT tries to grab food off your plate (you will be amazed at the reach your BT has).
- Your BT has the motor skills to pick objects up and place them in their mouth.

Good finger foods to experiment with

- Bread and cereal: low-sugar cereal pieces; cooked pasta shapes; fingers of toast or pitta bread.
- Dairy: small sticks of cheese.
- Fruit and vegetables: soft fruit, such as peeled apple and pear sticks, peach, pear or banana; cooked broccoli or cauliflower florets, green beans, carrot or courgette sticks.

How to relieve the pain of teething

Weaning often starts at the same time as teething, and this may affect your BT's appetite. Here are some tried and tested tips to help your BT through teething:

- Freeze feeding spoons and rub on sore gums.
- Give your BT a teething ring. Solid silicone-based teething rings are recommended over liquid-filled products, which could leak and can't be sterilised. You could try putting the teething ring in the fridge for a while before giving it to your BT.
- Serve food cool.
- Buy a mesh feeder. This is like a dummy with a mesh bag instead of a teat. You can put fruit and vegetables into the bag that your BT can chew on, but there is no choking risk. Do not consider giving your BT hard food to chew on unless it is in this type of feeder.

If your BT us clearly showing signs of discomfort that isn't relieved by any of the above, speak to your health visitor about administering sugar-free paediatric paracetamol.

COMMANDO DAD TOP TIP

Freeze flannels. They are excellent for teething BTs to chew on between meals. They are softer than teething rings, easier to hold and, if BTs accidentally hit themselves in the face with them, it won't hurt.

The importance of leading from the front and setting a good example

As your BT becomes an MT (and has more teeth and greater manual dexterity), you can start to give them bite-sized pieces of whatever you're eating.

Troopers learn by example, and will mimic your behaviour. Want them to eat the right amount of healthy nutritious foods? Then you need to do the same. If you tell your troopers that fruit and vegetables are delicious but they never see you eating them, you will fail.

★ ★ ★

A COMMANDO DAD ALWAYS ACTS IN THE BEST INTERESTS OF HIS TROOPERS

The golden rules of nutrition

- Take time for food.
- Understand portion sizes.
- Learn how to prepare nutritious foods for the unit.

Praise good eating habits. Your trooper will love the attention and will repeat the behaviour to get the same response.

The importance of taking time for food

Mealtimes are not only about food, but also socialising and enjoying each other's company. Ensure that your unit sits down together whenever possible – at least once a day. This relays the message, loud and clear, that:

- Eating is something pleasurable.
- You all belong to a secure and loving unit.

It will also enable you to demonstrate what good table manners are. It is too easy to rush food, especially with so many tasks to complete. Stop.

Do:

- Teach your troopers – and yourself – to slow down and enjoy food. It takes 20 minutes for the stomach to tell the brain that it is full. If you're racing your food, you won't pick up those messages, and as your troopers are following you, neither will they.

Don't:

- Put your troopers in a position where they rush their food and consequently overeat from an early age. This will cause problems later on. Big ones.

COMMANDO DAD TOP TIP

The preferred choice of drink at mealtimes is water. Make it the 'norm'. When the body is thirsty it requires water. Juice is high in sugar and should be limited. If juice is offered, ensure it is diluted one part juice to ten parts water.

The importance of portion sizes and a balanced diet

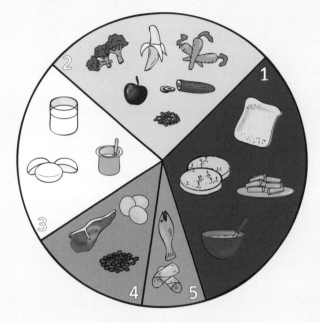

Portion size is critically important. A major cause of the obesity epidemic is that we have forgotten what a healthy portion size is, both for adults and troopers. The diagram shows the main food groups with examples of common foods and suitable portion sizes. See the *Resources* section on www.commandodad.com for more information about portion sizes for MTs.

The food groups

1. **Bread, cereals and potatoes**: these starchy foods, which also include pasta and rice, provide energy, fibre, vitamins and minerals.
2. **Fruit and vegetables**: provide fibre, vitamins and minerals and are a source of antioxidants.
3. **Milk and dairy foods**: provide calcium for healthy bones and teeth, protein for growth, plus vitamins and minerals.

4. **Meat, fish and alternatives**: these foods, which include eggs and pulses, provide protein and vitamins and minerals, especially iron. Pulses also contain fibre.

5. **Fats**: oils, dairy products, lean meats and oily fish are all good sources of fat-providing energy, omega 3 and vitamins A, D and E. Troopers up to the age of two years should be given full-fat products and not low-fat versions.

Note that processed foods, like biscuits, cakes, fizzy drinks, chocolate, sweets, crisps and pastries, do not fit into these groups. They contain high sugar and saturated fat levels and provide empty calories with no valuable nutrition. You know that these foods aren't good choices. Limit them.

COMMANDO DAD TOP TIP

Never overfill an MT's plate and bribe them to eat it. You may remember this as an effective tactic from your own childhood – but portion sizes have dramatically increased since then, and refined food is more common. An MT should only ever eat to fulfil hunger, not to please you. It is better to put too little on the plate and let your MT tell you when they want more.

How to prepare nutritious foods for the unit

Home-cooked foods are healthier than ready meals. You know this. Do not let this unnerve you. You may not think you have any skills in cooking. You will be relieved to discover how easy it is. It is not necessary to become a Michelin-starred chef but you do need to gain confidence and proficiency in basic cookery skills.

Frying tonight? Stop. A lot of food can just as easily be baked or grilled. If you fry more than twice a week, it is too much. Avoid fried food as much as possible for all BTs and MTs.

COMMANDO DAD TOP TIP

No food is bad. As long as you use your common sense, any food can have a place in your diet – and that of your troopers. Processed food and sweets should be limited but not completely banned. Banning specific foods will make them very, very desirable to your troopers – and you.

Here are some basic nutritious ideas that can be mixed and matched for a week's worth of meals. The only cookery skill you will need for the breakfasts and lunches is the ability to cook an egg. As your MT gets older, you should encourage them to help you prepare meals that require no cooking. For advice about meal routines see *Chapter 6: Standing Orders: Establishing Daily Routines.*

Good ideas for breakfast

Get into the habit of having a good, healthy, hearty meal at the start of the day. This will give you and your unit the energy (released slowly over the morning), and the right vitamins and minerals, needed to help you focus on the day's activities.

- Cereals such as porridge and muesli are good choices. Bran-based cereals can be too harsh on small digestive systems. Try to avoid chocolate- or sugar-covered cereals. They may contain additives and too much sugar and will not provide good quality energy for morning activities.

- Wholewheat toast, or bagel, with butter or margarine. Good toppings are: Marmite, peanut butter, cream cheese, sliced banana. Jam and marmalade are very popular, but use sparingly.

- Natural yogurt: a great way to get good bacteria into your MT. Ensure that they're not full of sugar. Can be served with chopped fruit or berries.

- Eggs are a really versatile breakfast item: boiled, scrambled, poached – find your MT's favourite.

- Continental breakfast can be popular too: cold meat and cheese with bread and butter.

- Pancakes with natural yogurt and fruit.

Good ideas for lunch

Remember, every MT is an individual; some may prefer a major feed-up at lunchtime and a lighter dinner, others a light lunch and a bigger dinner. Either way, preparing a meal with protein in the form of cheese, chicken, tinned tuna or other fish, beans, yogurt, etc., will keep them fuller for longer.

- A sandwich, on wholewheat bread or in a pitta, is a firm favourite. Fillings are endless – be inventive. Try toasting sandwiches for more variety.

- Wraps. As versatile as a sandwich and your MT will love the variety.

- A bowl of soup with wholewheat toast or bread.

- Low salt/low sugar beans are a versatile staple – try them on wholewheat toast, or with fish fingers or scrambled egg.

- Toasted wholewheat pitta bread cut into 'soldiers', cucumber and carrot batons, and hummus.

- Oatcakes with cheese and fruit.

- Lunch can be accompanied by fruit, easy for little fingers to cope with, such as sliced banana, chopped apple, cherry tomatoes, little satsumas, chopped pear, grapes and berries. Similarly, carrot, celery and cucumber, cut into batons, are popular vegetable choices.

Good ideas for dinner

These ideas require more cookery skill, but still nothing that you can't master. The idea is to make meals that the whole family can enjoy together. See the *Resources* section on www.commandodad.com for recipes and tips.

- Bangers and mash. A firm favourite for young and old. Get the best-quality sausages you can afford and grill or bake them. Watch salt levels especially in BTs under one.
- Home-made pizza. Buy pizza bases at the supermarket, spread with tomato paste and get your MT to top with their favourite toppings. Bake in the oven.
- Chicken (sliced chicken breast or baked thighs or drumsticks) and homemade oven-baked chips.
- Home-made tuna fishcakes with new potatoes and salad.
- Stew. Cut up plenty of fresh veg, fry meat briefly to seal the flavours in, add the vegetables and stock. Served with plenty of rice or mashed potato.
- Pasta dishes are popular dinner choices: pasta with home-made tomato or cheese sauce, spaghetti Bolognese and lasagne will become firm favourites, especially when served with garlic bread and salad.
- Roast dinner. So much easier than you think. Once the meat is in the oven, you only have to worry about preparing vegetables.
- Remember that every dinner does not have to be accompanied by a dessert. However, when you do need a dessert, good choices are jelly (easy to make – add frozen fruit to make it set quicker and add vitamins), bananas and custard, rice pudding (again, easy to make), fruit, yogurt (plain yogurt with honey – only give honey to troopers over a year old – and berries is a good choice), meringue nest with fruit and yogurt.

> # COMMANDO DAD TOP TIP
> A great time-saving gadget is a slow cooker. Meals can be prepared the night before, cooked throughout the day, and a healthy hot dinner will be ready at dinner time.

How to introduce variety to prevent boredom

Do:

- Help your trooper to discover different foods that will become new favourites. The more foods they try, the less likely they are to become picky eaters.
- Try to cook a completely new meal at least once a month. It can be fun to try new and interesting foods together.

Don't:

- Fall into a rut of preparing the same few meals – easy to do when you find out your trooper's 'favourites'.
- Feel you have to prepare a menu of new foods every week. It can be as simple as changing vegetables from carrots to sweetcorn, or replacing apples with pears, or giving oatcakes instead of bread and butter.

Lucky seven

Your BTs and MTs need to be exposed to a new food at least seven times before they can form an opinion about liking it – or not. Do not give up on healthy, nutritious foods too quickly. And never ever give up trying a healthy food before the seventh time because you don't like it.
Eat it seven times yourself. You may be surprised.

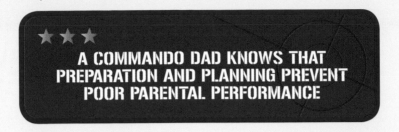

★ ★ ★

A COMMANDO DAD KNOWS THAT PREPARATION AND PLANNING PREVENT POOR PARENTAL PERFORMANCE

How to plan meals

Meal planning at the start of the week is important because it removes the stress of having to think through meals every day, and saves you money and time.

- Always check what you already have in your cupboards, fridge and freezer before planning the week's meals and writing a list.
- Keep a notebook for lists. Divide each sheet into four columns headed 'breakfast', 'lunch', 'dinner' and 'snacks' and write down under each the meals for the week. This is now your meal planner (and you can look at other weeks for inspiration). Write the list of ingredients you need underneath.
- Stick to your list. Do not buy on impulse.
- Make and freeze extra portions of home-cooked foods to save time, money and effort.
- **Read the label**. Don't believe a product is healthy because the marketing on the front tells you it is. If there is no 'traffic light' system on the label (where red is high, and green is low) look at the 'Per cent Daily Value' part of the 'Nutrition Facts' table to find out how much fat, sugar and salt it contains in one serving. Be aware that the labels are based on adult serving sizes, not MT serving sizes. For more information on the traffic light system, see *Resources* on www.commandodad.com.
- Do not shop when you are hungry. You will buy more than you need.

- If at all possible, leave all but the smallest BTs at home. It can be a challenging mission, even for you. Your excellent shopping list will keep the sortie as short as possible, but be aware that shopping can be a flashpoint for meltdowns, so see *Chapter 12: Dealing with Hostilities* for hints and tips.

COMMANDO DAD TOP TIP

Try to avoid chocolate bars, crisps, biscuits and sugary drinks for your basic survival kit. These are treats. They are also packed with sugar, additives, preservatives and plenty of 'empty' calories. They do not fill up your troopers (and so do not solve the hunger problem) and they are not what you – or your troopers – deserve or need.

How to prepare real food fast: healthy snacks

A Commando Dad is prepared for all eventualities. It's a universally acknowledged fact that ten minutes outside the safety of base camp, troopers will be hungry. Commando Dad doesn't question this; he embraces it and plans accordingly. The same rule applies when you have been away from base camp longer than anticipated and your troopers are starting to get hungry. You need food fast. You don't need fast food.

Below are some good food choices for your basic survival kit. Try them to see which works best for your troopers.

- Oatcakes.
- Small boxes of raisins.
- Fruit (apple, orange, grapes in a little pot, tomatoes, etc.)
- Vegetables (carrot batons, sugar snap peas, cucumber slices, etc.)
- Rice cakes.
- Dried fruit (pineapple/mango chunks, banana chips, etc.)
- Nuts (unsalted).
- Hummus.
- Small bottle of water or juice.
- Little container of favourite cereal.

COMMANDO DAD TOP TIP

Have a specific bag, lunchbox or small container as a designated snack pack for your basic survival kit. Check regularly. 'Fresh' foods need to be removed immediately on returning to the base camp. Failure to do so could render your kitbag US (unserviceable). Dried foods need to be checked to ensure that they are not stale. (Bite them. If soft things have gone hard, or hard things have gone soft, it's time to bin them.)

When having refs (refreshments) at home, snacks can include foods from the breakfast list, such as toast with peanut butter, or yogurt and berries. Chopped raw fruit and vegetables make an excellent snack and can be served with cheese or hummus for extra protein.

COMMANDO DAD TERMS USED IN THIS CHAPTER

Basic survival kit: a bag of everyday essentials. See *Chapter 4: Kitbags: Packing Everyday Essentials* for more details.

Base camp: home.

BT: baby trooper. A trooper (child) before it is mobile.

KFS: knife, fork, spoon; cutlery.

MT: mobile trooper. A trooper that can shuffle, crawl, stand up and, eventually, walk.

Refs: refreshment break.

Unit: family.

US: unserviceable.

CHAPTER 6:
STANDING ORDERS: ESTABLISHING DAILY ROUTINES

The brief:
A well-organised and fully functioning base camp runs on slick routines. Routine brings security, certainty and order, and makes life significantly more enjoyable for the whole unit. It is never too early – or too late – to establish routines.

Objective:
By the end of today's briefing you will have a greater understanding of the importance of the following routines; how to establish and maintain them; and routine 'flashpoints', where routines can break down, and how you can recover them.

- Feeding routine.
- Meal Routine.
- Good routines for morning, afternoon and evening.
- Weekend routine.
- Routine 'flashpoints'.

For routines associated with helping your BTs to sleep, including naps, see *Chapter 3: Sleep and Other Nocturnal Missions.*

Additional information can be found in the *Routine* section, under *Resources*, on www.commandodad.com.

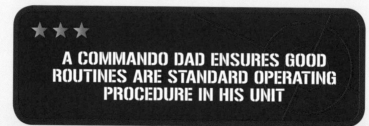

★ ★ ★

A COMMANDO DAD ENSURES GOOD ROUTINES ARE STANDARD OPERATING PROCEDURE IN HIS UNIT

COMMANDO DAD TOP TIP

Do not make your routine too rigid. It needs to be flexible enough to bend for different circumstances.

Feeding routine

For the first six weeks of your BT's life, they will need to be fed on demand.

Do:

- Ensure you and your partner eat well (see *Chapter 5: Nutrition: An Army Marches on its Stomach*) and rest whenever you can.
- Ignore the clock.

Don't:

- Put yourself or your partner under pressure to get into a routine for the first six weeks. Life has changed. You need time to adjust.
- Be unprepared when you bring your BT home. See *Chapter 1: The Advance Party: Preparing Base Camp*.

If your partner is breastfeeding, she will be in charge. Breast milk is digested really quickly, so she may be feeding your BT every two to three hours. Be there for support. If she can express milk with a breast pump, step up and take on night feeds.

When is the best time to introduce a feeding routine?
There are many different opinions, and methods, for the best way, and time, to do this. In this chapter I describe what worked for me and my three – very different – troopers.

After six weeks your BT can begin to establish a feeding routine. This will be helped by the fact you have already been helping them learn the difference between night and day, and that you have introduced other predictable activities. For more information, see *Chapter 3: Sleep and Other Nocturnal Missions*.

Your BT will have a natural rhythm for when they want to eat. Do not fight against it. Remember that a feeding routine should never be too rigid. Your BT's appetite will vary from day to day. Let them set the pace. Learn to decipher your BT's 'I am hungry' and 'I am full' cues. Breast feeding is recommended for the first six to twelve months, but all BTs are different and some might seem to require supplementary intake.

Common 'I am hungry' cues

- 'Rooting' when cradled (opening mouth and turning the head as if to breastfeed).
- Poking their tongue out.
- Sucking on their fists, or hands – or even clothes.
- Moving their head from side to side.
- Getting agitated, restless and fidgety.
- Crying (this is a pretty late signal).

Common 'I am full' cues

- Turning away from the breast or bottle.
- Lazy, slow sucking.
- Stopping sucking and looking up at you.
- Biting.

As your BT puts on weight, they will need fewer feeds, but will eat more each time. If your BT is happy, alert, filling nappies and sleeping well, they are getting enough to eat. If you have any concerns, speak to your health visitor.

It is normal for:

- Your BT to throw up a small amount after eating. It may not seem a small amount but it is all in the delivery. Make burping part of your routine to reduce this.

It is not normal for:

- Your BT to projectile vomit constantly after eating. Speak to your medical support crew: health visitor, doctor, nurse or pharmacist.

Meal Routine

Establish a set time to eat, and a meal routine to help meals run smoothly throughout the day.

MTs should:

- Help set and clear the table where appropriate.
- Be encouraged to go to the loo beforehand.
- Wash hands before eating.
- Sit down at the table when asked to do so.
- Follow the 'Table Rules' when eating. For example:

- No one goes AWOL (leaves the table without permission).
- Everyone sits properly on their seat.
- Everyone minds their Ps and Qs.

Reveille: morning routine

Preparing the night before

Make it a habit to prepare as much as you can before 'lights out'. Time flies in the morning and you don't want to be up at 0-silly-hundred-hours to get everything done.

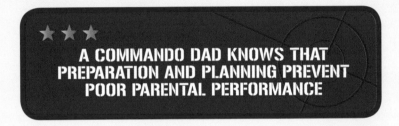

★ ★ ★

A COMMANDO DAD KNOWS THAT PREPARATION AND PLANNING PREVENT POOR PARENTAL PERFORMANCE

Also take into account the following day's activities, and pack and prepare accordingly. Do you have enough clean bottles? Have you replenished your basic survival kit? How long will you be away from base? What transport are you taking? What will the weather be like? Are there toilets and other facilities available? Will you be back at base before nap time?

Troopers in day nurseries

Ask your day nursery for a list of what your trooper will need. Label it. Pack it. Know how long it takes to get to your day-care centre, and allow at least ten minutes more than you think you will need once you are out of the door. If making a packed lunch, sandwiches are best made fresh in the morning, but other contents can be prepared the night before and stored in the fridge. Good ideas for healthy packed lunches can be found in *Chapter 5: Nutrition: An Army Marches on its Stomach*.

COMMANDO DAD TOP TIP

For BTs/MTs at day nursery, buy a notebook for staff to note down anything important and perhaps a few lines about the day's activities.

Waking-up routine

Have a set time for waking your troopers. Enter their bedroom in an upbeat and happy fashion; troopers take their cues from you. For troopers in nappies, change them straight away. If your MT is toilet-trained, or if you are in the process of toilet-training, encourage them to go to the loo before breakfast, and to flush and wash hands. For more advice on toilet-training, see *Chapter 9: Welcome to the Thunderbox: Toilet-training.*

Breakfast

If TV is part of your routine, leave it switched off until after breakfast. It will take your BT's/MT's attention away from eating. As with all meals, breakfast is an opportunity to spend time together.

Brushing teeth

Even before your BT has teeth, wipe their gums gently with a damp, soft cloth, wrapped around your finger. Do this after breakfast and before bed, to pave the way for the later brushing routine.

There is no set age for a BT to begin teething. Some BTs/MTs are born with them and some are over a year old before their first one appears. The average age for teeth to appear is six months. Your BT may not be average. Be vigilant. Once your BT starts to have teeth, you need to establish a teeth-brushing routine. For tips on how to relieve your BT's discomfort during teething, see *Chapter 5: Nutrition: An Army Marches on its Stomach.*

Do:

- Buy a soft brush with a small head.
- Buy special baby toothpaste.
- Only smear the brush with toothpaste. BTs only need a tiny amount.
- If your trooper has teeth, make sure you brush them before getting your trooper dressed. Toothpaste is a very stubborn stain to remove.

Don't:

- Brush too harshly.
- Expect your BT to gargle water or spit it out.
- Let your BT hold their toothbrush, yet. They don't have the dexterity to handle it. In the wrong hands a toothbrush is a formidable weapon.

As MTs get older, they may want to brush their own teeth. Encourage this, but MTs will not have the dexterity to ensure their teeth are cleaned properly. Let them 'start' or 'finish', with help from you.

COMMANDO DAD TOP TIP

Always encourage and praise your MT's attempts at independence: to dress themselves, to brush teeth, to tie laces, etc. Give them plenty of time because to small fingers, these tasks are a minefield. You will need to help, but don't just wade in. Ask them for permission to help them. If you don't, MTs may feel that they can't do it themselves. There is no place for learned helplessness in your base camp.

Getting kitted up

For MTs:

- This is a perfect opportunity to give older MTs the chance to practise important skills: putting on shirts, trousers, socks, etc., and the opportunity to deal with different types of fastenings.
- Give them plenty of time.
- Little competitions encourage your MT to stay on task: e.g. 'Can you beat yesterday's time?' 'How neat and tidy can you be today?'

COMMANDO DAD TOP TIP

In one specified place – ideally near the door – keep shoes, hats, coats, gloves, scarves, etc. Then your routine will never be derailed by unexpected weather conditions.

Afternoon routine

Use this routine whenever you are returning to base, and make sure to involve your MT as much as their age allows.

Returning to base camp

- If your MTs are enjoying an activity, give them a countdown to when the activity will end. They may still take departure badly. See *Routine flashpoints* later in this chapter for tips.
- Be sure to chat to your troopers on the way back to base camp, no matter how old they are.
- MTs will love to join in a conversation, BTs will love to listen to your voice, look at you and learn the tune of your language.

Returning from day nursery

- Ask teachers about your trooper's day, when they were last changed and fed.
- Make sure your trooper has all their kit.
- Chat to your troopers about their day on the way back to base camp. Even if your BT cannot reply, they will enjoy hearing the sound of your voice. Older MTs can share their successes and let off steam.

Entering base camp

- At the front door, take off shoes and coats and put them away.
- Put your kitbags and equipment away in the designated place.
- If MTs are in nappies, check if they need a new one. Do this even if they are asleep. Nappy rash ends up being painful for both of you.
- If your MT wears a uniform in day nursery, change them into mufti (plain clothes) immediately. If their uniform is clean, fold and put out ready for tomorrow. If not, put straight into the washing basket and ensure you have a clean uniform for the next day.
- Praise your MT if they kept their uniform or clothes clean, but don't criticise if their clothes are dirty. You want your MT to be active and adventurous, and dirty clothes can be the cost.

Depending on the time of your evening meal, you may want to give your MT a snack. Toast and fruit are good choices. For other snack ideas, see *Chapter 5: Nutrition: An Army Marches on its Stomach*.

Lights out: evening routine

For information about getting your BT into a sleep routine, see *Chapter 3: Sleep and Other Nocturnal Missions*.

Having a set bedtime is important, especially if BTs/MTs are in day nursery.

They may think they are not tired, but you know best.

An evening routine for BTs and MTs is really important because it gives them cues about what's coming next. Keep the mood as relaxed as possible. Here are some basic tips to ease the bedtime process.

- About an hour before bed, start calming down the atmosphere. Games should be finished (and no new ones started). If there is any tidying up to do, start it now, and get your MT to help.
- When tidying is complete, take your BT/MT for a bath or a wash.
- Dress your BT/MT for bed, letting MTs help to get themselves dressed.
- Decide whether you would like to take your trooper straight to bed or settle down with them for a few minutes on the sofa. Children's TV can be great at bedtime because it has stories designed to calm troopers down, which can act as a bedtime cue.
- Offer BTs a final feed and MTs a warm drink of milk (remembering that cow's milk is not suitable for BTs under six months old). It's a good bedtime cue and ensures they don't go to bed hungry.
- The final task before bedtime is teeth-brushing..
- Get your troopers into bed. A story can be a great way to settle your MTs (and BTs that are in a sleeping routine) but make sure it isn't too exciting. Speak slowly and calmly when reading the night-time story.

Weekend routine

The weekend gives Commando Dad and his troopers some well-earned time for R&R. Relaxation is important for you all. Life can be busy and it is good for your troopers to see you taking time to relax and just be together.

At the weekend exercise flexibility in relation to your established routines. Daily tasks such as getting-up times, mealtimes and dressing routines are all areas that can be relaxed. However, certain tasks should remain, whatever the day. For example, a toilet visit and hand-washing should precede mealtimes and teeth-brushing should follow breakfast and happen just before bed.

Plan your weekend activities beforehand. This allows you to make any special arrangements and sort out extra equipment or supplies you may need.

Routine 'flashpoints'

★ ★ ★

A COMMANDO DAD WILL IMPROVISE, ADAPT AND OVERCOME

'Flashpoints' can occur, even when a routine is slick and carried out to typical Commando Dad standards. The list below is not exhaustive, but it will give you some ideas of when flashpoints may occur and what you can do about them. These flashpoints may result in tantrums. See *Chapter 12: Dealing with Hostilities* for details about tantrums and how to avoid them.

- Overtiredness: just as with adults, when troopers get tired, they can get cranky. Be aware of how their behaviour changes, and, if necessary, take a rest break or change activity. Learn to spot the signals that your BT/MT is getting tired.
- Hunger or thirst: this can happen at any time. Commando Dad is prepared and will always have some healthy snacks and drinks (i.e. water) to hand.
- Overstimulation: BTs/MTs can get really excited, really quickly, but cannot calm down as fast. The most effective strategy is to break state by changing to a calmer activity.
- Changing a routine activity without letting your MT know beforehand. Routines are meant to be flexible but if you continually make changes, it is not a routine. BTs/MTs like routine because it makes them feel safe

and secure. If you need to change a routine activity, let them know beforehand.

- Disappointment. Sometimes your MT will be disappointed, for example, if you can't take them on an activity you had planned or if a visit from a much-loved relative is cancelled. Remain calm in the face of the invariably bad reaction. Disappointment is a big emotion and it can be hard for your MT to deal with, especially as they do not have the mental ability to simply 'look on the bright side'. You need to do that for them. Empathise and suggest another nice activity (which you must then follow through).

- Stopping BTs/MTs from doing an activity they enjoy. BTs/MTs are human. It is natural for them not to want to stop doing something they enjoy, but it is often necessary to keep to your routine. Try and give them a 'five-minute warning' or a countdown to when the activity needs to stop. Don't 'ambush' them at the last minute with a nasty surprise. Agree with your MT that they can continue later (or the following day). Follow through.

COMMANDO DAD TERMS USED IN THIS CHAPTER

0-silly-hundred-hours: very early, too early, in the morning.

AWOL: absent without leave; used to describe troopers leaving the table without permission.

Basic survival kit: a bag of everyday essentials. See *Chapter 4: Kitbags: Packing Everyday Essentials* for more details.

Base camp: home.

BT: baby trooper. A trooper (child) before it is mobile.

Mufti: non-uniform; plain clothes.

MT: mobile trooper. A trooper that can shuffle, crawl, stand up and, eventually, walk.

R&R: rest and recuperation.

Unit: family.

CHAPTER 7:
MORALE: A COMMANDO DAD'S SECRET WEAPON

The brief:

Parenting is a hugely important, responsible and, ultimately, rewarding job. However, at times it can feel like an isolating, unrewarding and thankless task. Build and maintain high morale so that, if 'down times' come, you are prepared.

Objective:

By the end of today's briefing you will have a greater understanding of:

- What morale is.
- How to recognise when your morale is under attack.
- How to build long-term morale.
- How to maintain morale in challenging situations.
- How to accept, and ask for, help.
- The importance of a support network.

What is morale?

Morale is difficult to put into words but easy to feel. If you have high morale you will feel confident, enthusiastic and motivated to do the task(s) at hand. High morale is important because it helps you to be an effective parent, which in turn builds your confidence and enthusiasm. If you have a bad day, you see it for what it is: one bad day. It will not affect your long-term view of yourself as a good, capable parent and you will still feel motivated to be the best dad you can be.

When you have low morale you may feel unable to cope or doubt your own abilities. A 'down day' will not be easily brushed off. It is difficult to be an effective parent in these circumstances.

You can start to improve your morale right now. Here's how:

How to build long-term morale

There are four cornerstones to building morale for a Commando Dad:

1. **Keep fit and healthy**: Parenting takes a lot of energy. Make sure that you give yourself a head start by eating well and exercising. When you have very young BTs/MTs at base camp, it's very difficult to get a full night's sleep. Establishing a sleep routine (enabling you to get as much sleep as possible) is very important. See *Chapter 3: Sleep and Other Nocturnal Missions* for more information.

2. **Perfect your routine**: A good routine, consistently executed, builds and maintains your sense of confidence and motivation. It reduces anxiety. It simply makes life easier.

3. **Use your support network**: There is not a lot of recognition for your hard work in parenting. Your MT will never thank you for a great day of parenting (any more than you thanked your own parents when you were an MT). It can seem like an unrewarding task. Your support network – family, friends and

like-minded individuals – can acknowledge and share your successes. They will also support you through challenging times. Do not underestimate the positive effect of belonging to a network.

4. Be kind to yourself: Parenting means facing new challenges and experiences. Some days you will get it right, and some days you will get it wrong. Continue to increase your skills but do not be overcritical of your own abilities. If your trooper is loved, physically safe and healthy, then you are doing a great job, and you are continuing to get better by the day.

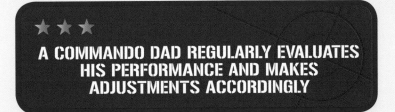

★ ★ ★

A COMMANDO DAD REGULARLY EVALUATES HIS PERFORMANCE AND MAKES ADJUSTMENTS ACCORDINGLY

COMMANDO DAD TOP TIP

Learn to understand the rule of sympathetic detonation – a chain reaction of emotions set off by you. If you are positive and happy, your kids will mirror this upbeat attitude. If you show them that you are upset, angry or frustrated, they will be too.

It is important to keep good morale in the unit. A caring and supportive relationship is the foundation. Your positivity will make your trooper feel secure; they know nothing can faze you and that you are in control.

> # COMMANDO DAD TOP TIP
> A family with high morale will have resilience, and the ability to bounce back. They will maintain an 'attitude of gratitude' and will always look on the bright side. This is a huge gift to give your trooper.

Maintaining morale in challenging situations

If your trooper sees you dealing with difficult situations with creativity and positivity, they will be confident that they can, too.

★ ★ ★

A COMMANDO DAD CANNOT HELP THE WAY HE FEELS BUT HE CAN HELP THE WAY HE ACTS

Three keys to maintaining morale in difficult situations:

- **Be prepared**: your consistent routine will take care of this.
- **Be positive**: rise above your present difficult situation, take the long-term view and stay positive.
- **Be resourceful**: use your imagination to come up with creative solutions to problems. Breaking state – doing something completely different – is a great way to change a negative situation quickly. Here are some tried and tested examples:
  - Stuck in a traffic jam and your troopers are in meltdown? Come off at the next exit and take the troopers to the park. BTs will enjoy the fresh air and change of pace, and MTs can run around.

- ○ A visit from a relative gets cancelled at the last minute? Call the parents of your MT's best friends to arrange an instant play date.
- ○ Raining? Have an indoor picnic. Build a tent by draping a sheet over the top of the table (or on the back of the sofa).

Some problems, however, cannot be solved by a quick solution. The golden rules to maintaining morale with your MTs in these situations are:

- Acknowledge that feelings of disappointment, anger and frustration are a natural response to a bad situation. Reassure MTs that things will get better.
- Empathise. Do not belittle your MT's feelings. For example, if a beloved pet dies, don't say, 'It was only a goldfish.' Acknowledge your MT's feelings and arrange a proper 'send-off'.
- Stick to your SOPs: it is comforting for the whole unit.
- Avoid comparisons. Some of your MTs bounce back quicker than others. This is natural. Give your MT the time they need.
- Encourage your MT to do any activity they enjoy, especially one they are good at. Positive feelings can have a miraculous effect on dealing with a negative situation.
- Do not use food to foster positive feelings, for example, by buying a sweet treat and assuring the MT they'll feel better when they've eaten it. You are teaching your MT that food can solve problems. It can't.
- Praise. It will reinforce your MT's s feelings of positivity.

How to accept – and ask for – help

Parenting is a 24/7 job, so accept help when it is offered, and ask for it when it is needed. This does not make you an inadequate parent. The most effective people in every field have a team of people working with them. Even the elite SAS – renowned for working alone – ensure they have support.

People want to help but often don't know what it is they need to do. If you are unaccustomed to asking for help you may not know what you need. Keep it practical. Here's a list of useful things that you could ask trusted friends and family to do for you:

- Bring food for that night's dinner. If you already have something prepared, freeze it.
- Pick up essential supplies on their way to your base camp: food, nappies, wipes, etc.
- Do light base-camp admin, such as wash up, put a wash load on, hang out washing, etc.
- Watch your BT/MT while you get some R&R: take a nap, do some personal admin (shower, shave and shampoo), or go for a walk.

COMMANDO DAD TOP TIP

When people ask to visit, make sure you arrange a time that is at YOUR convenience. Do not feel you have to entertain your visitors.

Advice

Lots of people will want to offer you advice. This can be a good thing, especially for the inexperienced parent. However, there is no 'one' way to bring up a child; every child is an individual. What works for one parent may not work for you. It may not even work for more than one of your BTs/MTs. Do not be afraid to try different things but also do not be afraid to stop doing what isn't working. Again, it's all about trial and error.

COMMANDO DAD TOP TIP

Be aware that people who get annoyed when you don't take their advice aren't giving you advice. They are giving you orders. You do not need to obey them.

Support networks

Letting off steam with people in the same boat as you can be an excellent coping mechanism, but it is not an effective long-term strategy. You do not need to constantly be discussing and bemoaning how hard it is to be a parent. You know how hard it is. What you need are excellent and effective strategies that will make the experience enjoyable and rewarding.

You need to find, or create, a group of like-minded individuals who are as positive and enthusiastic about parenting as you are. The people in this 'support network' need to be all moving towards the same goal: being the best parents you can be and raising happy, healthy, responsible BTs/MTs to be proud of. When you feel low, their enthusiasm will inspire you and vice versa.

Good places to look for support and impartial advice include:

- NCT: www.nct.org.uk
- Baby Centre: www.babycentre.co.uk
- NHS Choices: www.nhs.uk
- www.commandodad.com
- www.mumsnet.com/talk/dadsnet

Birds of a feather flock together: i.e. like-minded individuals attract each other. Perhaps you have friends that are already parents or 'expecting'. Go to local parenting groups. You will find them in your local paper, and in ads in community places, such as doctors' surgeries or libraries, and online. You will find the individuals that you want to have in your support network, and they will find you.

COMMANDO DAD TERMS USED IN THIS CHAPTER

Base camp: home.
Base-camp admin: housework.
BT: baby trooper. A trooper (child) before it is mobile.
Personal admin: shower, shave and shampoo.
R&R: rest and recuperation.
SOPs: standard operating procedures.
Sympathetic detonation: a chain reaction of emotions set off by you.
Unit: family.

CHAPTER 8

CALL THE MEDIC: BASIC FIRST AID AND UNIT MAINTENANCE

The brief:
For troopers, life is a battlefield of bumps, bruises and bugs. You need to learn how to distinguish between a common ailment and a more serious issue that requires immediate assistance. The information below is my suggested advice only. If you are ever in doubt about your BT's/MT's health or well-being, seek medical advice from your medical support team.

Objective:
By the end of today's briefing you will have a greater understanding of common – and more serious – trooper ailments, and how to deal with them.

- How to assemble a basic first aid kit for your BT/MT.
- High temperatures: how to recognise and deal with them.
- Minor combat injuries: how to deal with them.
- Common trooper ailments: how to recognise and deal with them.
- Conditions that require immediate action: signs and symptoms.

★ ★ ★

A COMMANDO DAD WILL TAKE CARE OF HIS UNIT WITH ALL MEANS AT HIS DISPOSAL.

COMMANDO DAD TOP TIP

Taking a paediatric first aid course will increase your skill and confidence. Find your nearest provider by trying an Internet search, or asking your health visitor, doctor's receptionist or at your local library.

How to assemble a basic first aid kit for your BT/MT

The golden rules of assembling a BT/MT first aid kit:

- Your first aid kit should always be readily accessible but out of your trooper's reach.
- Check your kit monthly to replenish and replace expired medications.
- Have a designated box and always keep it in the same place.

Your basic trooper first aid kit: core kit

- Sachets of paediatric paracetamol and paediatric ibuprofen (bottles are too messy). Check the label to ensure your trooper meets the weight and age requirements before administering.
- A selection of plasters. Attractive plasters aid rapid healing.
- Finger bandage.
- Antiseptic cream, also suitable for stings and bites.
- Antiseptic wipes.

Hardware

- Thermometer.
- Medicine spoon or baby syringe (to administer the medicine).
- Tweezers.
- Scissors.

Useful additions (can be bought as and when needed)

- Cotton wool balls and cotton buds.
- Instant cold pack.
- Saline solution and eye bath.
- Sachets of rehydration salts (to replace the salts and minerals lost through diarrhoea and vomiting). Only to be used on the advice of your doctor.
- Calamine lotion.

High temperatures: how to recognise and deal with them

For MTs under five, a temperature over 37.5°C (99.5°F) is considered high. Your trooper's face may be flushed and will feel hot to the touch.

High temperatures – or fevers – can be caused by your trooper's body fighting off an infection, but also by:

- Overheating: is your trooper overdressed for the conditions? Remove extra layers, wait 20 minutes and take their temperature again.
- Teething.
- A recent vaccination.

COMMANDO DAD TOP TIP

I found the best way to take my trooper's temperature was using a digital thermometer in the armpit. It's the least intrusive method and results are fast and accurate.

How to take a temperature reading with a digital thermometer

Read manufacturer's instructions before you need to use it.

- Turn on the thermometer and make sure the screen is clear of old readings.
- This is a two-hand operation. Lie your trooper down or sit them in a seat.
- Place the tip of the thermometer on the bare skin in the middle of your trooper's armpit.
- Use one hand to hold the thermometer and the other to hold your trooper's arm still, for about 15 seconds.

How to deal with a high temperature

Do:

- Try to reduce a temperature with paediatric paracetamol.
- Always adhere to dosage instructions.
- Keep your BT/MT hydrated. Encourage them to drink little and often.

Don't:

- Give your MT food, unless they ask for it.

If you are concerned by your trooper's high temperature, seek professional help. Ring NHS Direct or your doctor's surgery for advice on next steps.

Minor combat injuries and how to deal with them

When administering any treatment to your trooper, be calm and compassionate. Speak in a soothing voice.

Bumps and bruises (BT/MT)

- Cold may diminish discomfort and the size of the bump or bruise.
- Apply a cold compress (e.g. a cold washcloth, gel pack, frozen peas, ice in a tea towel).
- If the skin is broken, clean carefully with an antiseptic wipe or sterile (i.e. boiled, then cooled) water.
- Be gentle: skin will be tender and sore.

Cuts (BT/MT)

- Wash the area with an antiseptic wipe or sterile water.
- If the cut is bleeding, apply direct pressure. Use a clean, soft gauze pad. Press the skin together as you gently push down on the cut. Check after a minute to determine if the bleeding has stopped.
- When the cut is no longer bleeding, allow the area to air-dry and apply antiseptic cream and then a dressing (or plaster, depending on the size of cut).
- If your trooper's cut won't stop bleeding, or fails to show signs of healing, or if there is redness, swelling or pus anywhere near the site of the cut, seek professional help. Ring NHS Direct or your doctor's surgery for advice on next steps.

Bites and scratches: animal (BT/MT)

- On initial impact clean the wound thoroughly with antiseptic wipes or sterile water and apply antiseptic cream.
- If the skin has been broken with an animal bite, even if it appears minor, ring your doctor.
- If the wound is large or deep, ring your doctor immediately to see if they have the facilities to deal with your trooper on site. If not, take your trooper to A & E immediately.
- All animal bites and scratches propose a high risk of infection and medical advice should be sought if experienced.

Bites and stings: insect (BT/MT)

- If the sting is visible carefully scrape it off with something blunt, e.g. the blunt edge of a bank card. Do not try and squeeze it out or pull it out with tweezers, as this can spread the poison.
- Apply a cold compress for ten minutes.
- If your trooper has been stung in the mouth, give them an ice cube to suck on, or cold water to drink.
- If your trooper shows signs of a serious allergic reaction, which include difficulty breathing, swelling of the face, throat or mouth, or wheezing, call 999.

Stings: nettle (BT/MT)

- Look for a dock plant (large plant with very broad, green leaves) near the nettle plant and rub a dock leaf on the sting.
- If there are no dock leaves available, apply some nappy-rash cream from your basic survival kit.

Nosebleed (BT/MT)

- Sit your trooper down and tip their head forward.

- Ask MTs to breathe through their mouth and give them a cloth to catch blood drips. Wipe the blood from your BT's face using a clean, soft cloth.
- Gently nip the nose (just above the nostrils) between your thumb and index finger.
- Hold the nose for ten minutes.

If the nose will not stop bleeding, or if your trooper has frequent nosebleeds, call the doctor. If you suspect that your trooper's nose is broken, ignore these steps and take them straight to A & E.

Common trooper ailments: how to recognise and deal with them

Colic (BT)

Symptoms

- Frequent waking during the night.
- Inconsolable crying which starts in the evening.
- Discomfort that is seemingly due to trapped wind.

Treatment

- There is no medical cure for colic.
- Ensure you burp BTs properly during a feed. Follow your favoured burping method during an attack.
- Movement is soothing and can reduce distress: walk with your BT, rock them from side to side.
- If your BT is breastfed, your partner needs to avoid food that could cause wind.

Colds (BT/MT)

Symptoms

- A runny nose.
- Sneezing.
- A cough.
- High temperature.
- Gradual onset of above symptoms.

Treatment

- Keep your trooper hydrated.
- Give your trooper plenty of rest.
- Treat the temperature with paediatric paracetamol.
- If your trooper wants to eat, give them healthy, fresh foods.
- Look out for secondary infections and treat those accordingly.
- Keep hands clean to prevent germs from spreading.

Croup (BT)

Symptoms

- A barking cough.
- A hoarse throat.
- Rapid breathing.

Treatment

- Reduce your BT's distress by soothing and comforting them.
- Keep your BT hydrated.
- Use paediatric paracetamol to reduce a temperature.

If your BT's symptoms get worse, or if your BT is fighting for breath, call 999 or take them straight to A & E.

Ear infections (BT/MT)

Symptoms

- High temperature.
- Diarrhoea.
- Ear tenderness.
- MTs may be unsteady on their feet and pull at their ear.
- Occasionally blood or offensive discharge coming out of the affected ear (the eardrum has burst).

Treatment

- Seek a medical evaluation from your doctor, as medicine may be needed.
- Never, ever put any object (such as cotton buds) in your BT's ear.
- If there is blood and pus coming out of your BT's ear, clean it away with cotton wool balls and sterile water. Call your doctor immediately. If you are not able to be seen, ring NHS Direct for advice on next steps. Keep hands clean to prevent germs from spreading.

Eye infections and blocked tear ducts (BT)

Symptoms

- Very watery eyes.
- Red, sore eyes.
- A discharge from the eye.
- 'Crusty' eyes on waking.

Treatment

- Seek a medical evaluation from your doctor, as medicine may be needed.
- Incorrect use of eye drops can cause damage to the eye and therefore they should only be administered on medical advice. When they blink, BTs will spread the medicine throughout the eye.

- If there is a discharge, or if your BT has 'crusty' eyes, clean the eye using a cotton wool ball with sterile water.
- Wipe the eye across from tear duct to outer edge.
- Strictly only one wipe per cotton wool ball. Eye infections are highly contagious.
- Keep hands clean to prevent germs from spreading.

Flu (BT/MT)

Symptoms

- High temperature.
- Aching joints.
- Chills.
- Runny nose.
- Cough.
- Sore throat.
- Rapid onset of above symptoms.

Treatment

- As for a cold.
- Use paediatric paracetamol and paediatric ibuprofen to relieve aches and pains.

If your trooper has a very high temperature and you are unable to bring it down, seek professional help. Call your doctor immediately. If you are not able to be seen, ring NHS Direct for advice on next steps.

Highly infectious viral illnesses: e.g. measles and chickenpox (BT/MT)

Symptoms

- Chickenpox: Red, itchy spots that quickly (within 24 hours) blister and scab.

- Measles: red-brown spotty rash, with spots often joined together, and flu-like symptoms.

Treatment

- Contagious troopers need to be isolated from other troopers (and pregnant women) as soon as possible.
- Seek a medical evaluation from your doctor, as medicine may be needed.
- Calamine lotion applied to rashes may help reduce itching.
- Keep troopers hydrated.
- Use paediatric paracetamol to reduce a high temperature.
- Keep hands clean to prevent germs from spreading.

Constipation (BT/MT)

Symptoms

- Infrequent or very large stools with a hard consistency.
- High temperature.
- Stomach ache and discomfort.
- Long time between visits to the thunderbox.
- Difficulty or distress when passing stools.

Treatment

- Increase trooper's fluid intake.
- Consult your health visitor, pharmacist or family doctor for advice.

If you don't already provide your trooper with a diet rich in fresh vegetables and fruit, make diet adjustments now.

Cradle Cap (BT/MT)

Symptoms

- Thick, yellowish skin that may look like scales, on your BT's head.

Treatment

- Rub a few drops of olive oil between your fingers and gently massage into the cradle cap.
- Add more oil if needed but always to your fingers first, and a few drops at a time.
- Wash your BT's hair with mild shampoo, twice.
- Using a soft baby brush, or soft dry flannel, brush away loose scales.

Dehydration (BT/MT)

Symptoms

- Fewer than 3–4 wet nappies a day.
- Crying with little or no tears.
- BT: a sunken fontanelle.
- Weight loss.
- Dry lips.

Treatment

- Increase your trooper's fluid intake immediately (in addition to but not in substitution for normal feeds). With BTs up to six months old tap water should never be used as a supplementary fluid.
- If symptoms persist, make an immediate appointment at the doctor's.

Diarrhoea (BT/MT)

Symptoms

- Very loose, frequent stools.

- Mucus or blood in your trooper's loose stools.

Treatment

- Change nappies quickly and clean the area with mild wipes or cotton wool and sterile water.
- If you see mucus or blood in your trooper's stools, make an immediate appointment at the doctor's.
- Keep hands clean to prevent germs from spreading.

Nappy rash (BT)

Symptoms

- Red and inflamed skin around the bottom.

Treatment

- Change nappies quickly and clean the area with mild wipes or cotton wool and sterile water.
- Let air get to the rash and help dry it out. At base camp, let your BT roll around on a clean towel without a nappy.
- Apply nappy-rash cream from your basic survival kit. If your BT is prone to nappy rash, you may want to use this cream every time you change their nappy.

Vomiting (BT/MT)

Symptoms

- Explosive and persistent vomiting.
- A distressed BT (BTs are usually OK with throwing up food so this may be an indication of another problem).

Treatment

- For BTs, make burping part of your feeding routine. This will reduce food-related vomiting and make sure that you are not overfeeding your BT.
- If vomiting occurs with diarrhoea or fever, it could be the sign of another illness, such as an infection. Look for other symptoms and treat accordingly.
- Keep hands clean to prevent germs from spreading.

If you are unable to stop explosive vomiting within 24 hours, make your trooper an immediate appointment at the doctor's. If you are unable to get an appointment, call NHS Direct for further advice and guidance.

Conditions that require immediate action: signs and symptoms

If your trooper displays symptoms of meningitis or pneumonia, call 999 or take them straight to A & E. Do not delay. A doctor needs to make the diagnosis quickly.

Meningitis (BT/MT)

- Bacterial meningitis:
  - Fever.
  - Floppy and unresponsive.
  - Irritable.
  - Vomiting.
  - Loss of appetite.
  - Pale, blotchy skin.
  - A staring expression.
  - Very sleepy and hard to rouse.
  - BTs only: swelling in the front of the head (fontanelle).

- A purplish or red rash. If you press a clear glass tumbler firmly against the rash, and you can still see the rash through the glass, your trooper may have septicaemia (blood poisoning). Call 999 or take your trooper to A & E.
  - Rapid onset of above symptoms.
- Viral meningitis:
  - Mild flu-like symptoms.
  - Neck stiffness.
  - Muscle or joint pain.
  - Nausea and vomiting.
  - Diarrhoea.
  - Sensitivity to light.
  - Rapid onset of above symptoms.

Pneumonia (BT/MT)

- Coughing.
- Fever.
- Rapid breathing (more than 30 to 40 breaths a minute).
- Skin appears to sink between their ribs when they breathe.

```
COMMANDO DAD TERMS
USED IN THIS CHAPTER
```

Base camp: home.
BT: baby trooper. A trooper (child) before it is mobile.
MT: mobile trooper. A trooper that can shuffle, crawl, stand up and, eventually, walk.
Thunderbox: toilet.

CHAPTER 9:

WELCOME TO THE THUNDERBOX: TOILET-TRAINING

The brief:
Toilet-training is a big transition for your MT. You need to approach it in an upbeat fashion and make it as pleasant an experience as possible. You may have hiccups along the way, but keep your eye on the prize: you are on the threshold of being free of daytime nappies and all their associated admin.

Objective:
By the end of today's briefing you will have a greater understanding of how you can best help your MTs to master the Thunderbox.

- Toilet-training: what it is and how, and when, to deal with it.
- Recognising your MT's cues.
- The golden rules of toilet-training.
- Essential kit list for toilet-training.
- Toilet-training routines.

COMMANDO DAD TOP TIP
Keep upbeat and positive. If you get stressed, so will your MT, and this could discourage them from using the thunderbox. You do not want your MT to hold it in as this could cause discomfort and lengthen the time it takes to toilet-train. For more information on constipation and how to deal with it, see *Chapter 8: Call the Medic: Basic First Aid and Unit Maintenance.*

Toilet-training: what it is and how, and when, to deal with it

Toilet-training is when your MT learns to master their bodily functions and can 'hold on' until they get to a toilet. It is sometimes referred to as being dry.

Recognising your MT's cues

As you will know by now, every MT is different. There is no set time when your MT is ready to begin thunderbox training. Look out for the following cues from about 18 months:

- Your MT's bowel movements become more regular.
- Your MT is aware of when they are filling their nappy (and they may choose to be away from company as they fill it).
- Your MT tells you when they have filled their nappy and needs to be changed.
- Increasingly dry nappies during the day (MTs may need night-time nappies for years after they have mastered the thunderbox).

The golden rules of toilet-training

Do:

- Prepare for little accidents by taking extra clothes and wipes (you will already have one full set of clothes in your basic survival kit) if on a sortie, and having appropriate cleaning supplies at base camp.

- Be relaxed. Be calm. It's only poo.

- Create a routine that involves flushing the loo, putting the toilet lid down, and washing and drying hands, even if your MT doesn't manage to use the thunderbox. This not only promotes good hygiene but also ensures that, no matter what else happens, the MT can successfully complete his routine.

- Praise, praise, praise. Even when your MT doesn't manage to use the thunderbox, praise them for trying.

- Dress your MT in clothes that they can easily get out of by themselves, and invest in training pants (a nappy that can be pulled up and down like pants).

- Let your MT see you using the loo and explain what you're doing.

Don't:

- Get upset or angry about accidents. MTs take their cues from you and anger and upset will not help them master this new skill.

- Constantly ask them if they need to go, and make an issue out of it. But do ask them at regular intervals – when you are going to the thunderbox, or around the time you expect them to need to have a bowel movement for example – if they'd like to use the thunderbox.

- Feel that you or your MT has failed if, after successfully being 'dry', they start to have accidents. It's perfectly natural for this to occur. If your MT starts to get upset by the situation, it is fine to put them back in nappies for a while.

- Put pressure on your MT to stay dry in the night. Night-time nappies will need to be worn until an MT can keep them dry for at least a week. It is not unusual for MTs to wear night-time nappies right up until they are seven years old.

- Persist if your MT is not keen, or even worse, upset. They will use the thunderbox when they are ready.
- Feel there is something wrong with your parenting if your MT's peers are dry before they are. Thunderbox training is not a competitive sport.

COMMANDO DAD TOP TIP

Whether to use a potty is a personal preference, but I went straight to a toilet-training seat with my MTs. I simply could not think of another place in the base camp I would rather have them take a poo than the thunderbox.

Essential kit list for toilet-training

You don't require a great deal of kit, but make sure your 'G10 store' is fully stocked and replenish regularly.

- Potty or toilet-training seat (a special seat that fits inside a regular toilet seat, meaning your MT goes straight on to the toilet).
- Splash mat if you intend to use a potty.
- Toilet step if you are going for the toilet-training seat.
- Training pants for the early stages.
- Loose-fitting clothing that is easy for your MT to undo by themselves.
- Flushable wipes.
- Appropriate supplies for cleaning up accidents.
- Night-time nappies.

Toilet-training routine

As in all other areas, Commando Dad looks to establish an effective routine when thunderbox-training. The routine that worked for me is detailed below. Tailor it to work with your own MT.

- If using a potty, make sure it is always clean and in the same place (preferably in the thunderbox).
- Let your MT undress themselves. Be sure to offer help, especially if you think you might be in accident territory, but do not take over.
- If your MT does have an accident, make it clear that it is not a problem, and calmly take the clothes to the dirty-washing basket.
- If your MT goes in the thunderbox, encourage them to wipe themselves (with your help).
- If using a toilet-training seat, close the toilet lid and flush.
- If using a potty, put the contents of the potty straight down the toilet, close the lid and flush.
- Wash and dry both yours and your MT's hands.

COMMANDO DAD TERMS USED IN THIS CHAPTER

Basic survival kit: a bag of everyday essentials. See *Chapter 4: Kitbags: Packing Everyday Essentials* for more details.

Base camp: home.

G10 store: a place in base camp where you store all of the essential equipment.

MT: mobile trooper. A trooper that can shuffle, crawl, stand up and, eventually, walk.

Thunderbox: toilet.

Unit: family.

CHAPTER 10:
ON MANOEUVRES:
TRANSPORTING THE TROOPS

The brief:
Manoeuvres are an essential part of everyday life. Ensure that when you are transporting the troops, you are prepared for anything, and that your troops are safe and accounted for at all times.

Objective:
By the end of today's briefing you will have a greater understanding of:

- Transporting your troopers on foot:
  - Baby carriers.
  - Pushchairs.
  - Travel systems.
  - Reins.
  - Buggy boards.
- Transporting your troopers by car:
  - Car seats.
  - Car survival kit.
  - Car first aid kit.
- Transporting your troopers on public transport:
  - Bus or tram.
  - Coach.
  - Train.
  - Aeroplane.
  - At the airport.
  - During the flight.

★ ★ ★

**A COMMANDO DAD PUTS THE
SAFETY OF HIS TROOPERS AT THE
HEART OF ALL TRAVEL PLANS**

The golden rules of troop transportation

- Travel equipment for BTs/MTs is big business. From baby carriers to travel systems, you will find many brands, many styles, many features and many prices.
- Do not be seduced by anything other than its suitability for your lifestyle.
- Look at the key considerations below to help you make the right decisions.

Transporting your troopers on foot

adjustable shoulder straps

adjustable waist straps

lightweight carrier

I found that baby carriers were a great solution for transporting very young BTs. Baby carriers hold your BT against your body but leave your hands free for your many other tasks. Other advantages are:

- Your BT will feel warm and secure.
- The physical closeness may help you bond with each other.
- It doesn't entail any bulky equipment.
- When your BT is old enough to hold their head unsupported (by about six months), some models enable you to turn your BT around so they can face the world.

Ease of use

- Are you able to easily fasten and unfasten the clasps?

Practicality

- Is it comfortable for you? As a general rule, the wider the straps, the better.
- Is it comfortable for your BT? Your BT's head and trunk should not be unsupported in any way, but of course their arms and legs can be out of the carrier.
- Are you able to easily wash it?

Value

- How often do you plan to use the carrier? Is the investment worth it?

Do:

- Shop around and take time to find a baby carrier that suits you.
- Practise opening and closing fastenings, before your BT is in the carrier.

Don't:

- Travel in a car with your BT in a carrier – it is dangerous and illegal. BTs must be secured in a car seat.
- Overdress your BT. It is easy for BTs to get hot, so dress them in light layers.

A **pushchair** can last you from birth to the toddler stage, if you choose wisely. Think of it like buying a car: you must try these wheels before you buy.

Ease of use

- Is it easy to assemble? Can you do it one-handed (you may have your BT in the other hand)?
- Is it easy to manoeuvre? Can you manoeuvre it with one hand?
- If you are tall, can you adjust the height of the handles to make the pushchair easier for you to push?

Practicality

- If it will be your primary mode of transport, does it have a basket underneath for shopping and supplies?
- Will you have to get it up and down often? How heavy is it? How bulky is it?
- Will it easily fit in your car boot or your house when it is not in use?
- Is it wider than the average shop door?

Value

- Does it come with the essential 'extras' (sun visor, rain cover, etc.), or do you need to buy these separately?

COMMANDO DAD TOP TIP

Pushchairs are a big investment. Consider second-hand models. Good places to look for second-hand pushchairs are classified ads in local newspapers, noticeboards in newsagents/ supermarkets, eBay and Freecycle. Freecycle is an online community where unwanted belongings are given good homes (and kept out of landfill) for free. See www.freecycle.org. Exercise normal levels of caution if buying on eBay. Always check the safety/roadworthiness of your purchase.

For more tips on choosing a pushchair, or a double pushchair, see *Resources* on www.commandodad.com.

Travel systems are a combination of car seat and pushchair, and usually include a carrycot (which effectively converts the pushchair into a pram).

Ease of use

- Is it easy to disassemble?
- Is it easy to manoeuvre?
- Can you adjust the height of the handles?

Practicality

- Does it meet all the criteria you would demand of each individual item?
- Does the car seat fit easily in your car?

Value

- Would you have bought all the items individually: pushchair, car seat (that will need to be replaced within a year) and carrycot?

- The pram is really only useful as a means of transport until your BT can sit up, although it may be possible to use the carrycot as a first bed for your BT.
- Do all the parts come as standard, or do you need to buy the car seat separately?

MTs want to, and should be encouraged to, walk. **Reins and wrist straps** are an ideal way to give your toddling MT more independence while keeping them safe. Reins come with a harness or backpack that your MT wears; the reins run from the harness or backpack to your wrist. The advantages of this method of transport are:

- It can be useful when your MT is still unsteady on their feet.
- Your MT will have no road sense. You can use reins to keep them on the pavement.
- It can provide an extra layer of protection in crowded places where your MT might slip your hand.

Ease of use

- Will they fit under your pushchair or in your rucksack until you need them?

Practicality

- Will your MT be happy to wear them? Try before you buy.

Value

- Will you use them? Is it worth investing in some?

COMMANDO DAD TOP TIP

MTs can get tired very quickly, and like to bimble. For these reasons, do not set unrealistic expectations in terms of distance for your MT to walk. If you do, be prepared to carry your tired MT, or bring along an alternative method of transport to get you both back to base camp.

Buggy boards are great when your MT has reached their yomping limit, and there's a BT in the pushchair. A buggy board is a wide step that attaches to the back of the pushchair for your MT to stand on.

Ease of use

- Can you easily get it on and off your model of pushchair?

Practicality

- Will your MT be happy to travel on it? Try before you buy.

Value

- Will you use it? Is it worth investing in one?

Transporting your troopers by car

A **car seat** is an essential – and legal – requirement for troop transportation by car.

Ease of use

- Can you easily get it in and out of your car? When familiar with your child restraint, fitting will take 30 seconds. Ensure you are shown how to fit the seat correctly by trained assistants when buying, to make this job easier and most importantly safe for each journey.
- Is it heavy, even without your BT in it?

Practicality

- Does it fit your car? Good shops will offer to fit the car seat in your car. Let them, but note how they do it. Then practise.
- Does it provide your child with adequate support while giving them room to grow?
- Is it safe? Does it conform to British Standards and carry the BSI 'Kitemark' or the European 'CE' mark?

- Can you remove the covers and wash them?

Value

- How long will your trooper be able to use the model you are considering?

Hand-me-down car seats from your older MTs, or from friends and relatives, are fine provided they have **never** been damaged (or been involved in a car accident). Also check that they conform to the standards as mentioned above and no parts are missing. If the instructions have been lost, request replacements from the manufacturer to ensure you are familiar with how it works. If in doubt, seek professional advice.

In addition to a well-fitted and safe car seat, the car should contain the following:

Car survival kit

This will be kept in your glove compartment or the side door, and can be left in the car at all times. It will rescue the situation if you forget your basic survival kit for light-order missions.

- Wipes (small pack or a few wipes in a sandwich bag).
- Nappies (x 2).
- One change of clothes.
- 1 x nappy sack or plastic bag.

Car first aid kit

It is not mandatory to carry a first aid kit in your car, but I highly recommended it. It is possible to buy first aid kits for the car, or you can make your own. This kit must contain:

- Torch.
- Foil blanket.
- Cold pack.
- Plasters.

- Bandages.
- Tape/safety pins.
- Dressings.
- Antiseptic cream.
- Age-appropriate painkillers.

For more information on first aid, see *Chapter 8: Call the Medic: Basic First Aid and Unit Maintenance*. For strategies on amusing your troopers during car journeys, see *Chapter 11: Entertaining the Troops*.

Transporting your troopers on public transport

Travelling by public transport is straightforward but requires planning.

- Recce your route to the station or stop. Give yourself at least ten minutes more time than you may think you need to get there. Know your timetable.
- Avoid travelling at peak times if possible. Public transport is far less stressful, and often cheaper, during off-peak hours.
- Check accessibility at your departure and arrival station or stops. Look for wheelchair access signs, because if you have a pushchair, your accessibility needs are the same.

Bus or tram

If you travel with a pushchair, you may face some challenges because:

- Most buses or trams have steps.
- Doors may be too narrow for a pushchair, meaning you will have to collapse the pushchair with one hand, and carry it on the bus or tram (unless you are travelling with another adult).
- You have to get on the vehicle, pay (or show a pass) and find a seat while holding your BT, a pushchair, and other supplies. Ideally before the bus or tram starts to move.

These challenges can be overcome with experience and organisation:

- Ask for help getting on and off the vehicle. The public will often willingly help when asked (I have never been refused), but the natural reserve of the British means that people are simply too shy to offer.
- ALWAYS apply the brakes of your pushchair.
- Alert the driver that your stop is approaching by ringing the bell, and then wait for the bus to stop before you unbrake the pushchair and make your way to the front of the bus.

For strategies on amusing your troopers during bus and tram journeys, see *Chapter 11: Entertaining the Troops.*

Coach

This is not as challenging as travelling by bus because:

- You have a designated seat and you can stow away a lot of your kit (remember that the basic survival kit for light-order missions should not be stored in the underneath storage compartment of the coach).
- You have more time to get on and off the coach.

However, you may need to ask for help, as the steps are typically very narrow.

For strategies on amusing your trooper during coach journeys, see *Chapter 11: Entertaining the Troops.*

Train

In addition to checking station accessibility, the main challenge with train travel is the gap between the train and the platform edge. As with bus or tram travel:

- Remember to apply the brakes of your pushchair when the train is in motion.
- Ask for help getting on and off the train.
- For short journeys, stand by the train doors as this area is wide enough not to have to collapse your pushchair.

- For long journeys, collapse your pushchair and store it in the luggage compartment at the end of the carriage.

For strategies on amusing your trooper during train journeys, see *Chapter 11: Entertaining the Troops*.

Aeroplane

Do not shy away from the challenge of keeping troops seated, quiet and entertained for prolonged periods of time. Do not be phased by troop meltdown, but remain calm and prepared for all outcomes. Always check rules and restrictions beforehand with the travel agent or airline. Turning up at the airport to find bags are wrongly packed, overweight or oversized is not a smart move.

At the airport

- Get to the airport early. Do not put the unit under additional stress by having to rush around unfamiliar territory.
- Prepare beforehand:
  - Book seats online and print out boarding passes.
  - Put together an emergency contact list, including details of the British Embassy or High Commission at your destination (if you are travelling abroad).
  - Get foreign currency if needed. Be aware that the exchange rates at the airport are the least favourable.
  - Familiarise yourself with your destination: maps, information about hotels, etc.
  - Ensure passports are in date. Check the criteria for travel to your destination. For example, entry to the US now requires a passport with at least six months' validity, as well as pre-registration on the ESTA (Electronic System for Travel Authorization) system. For more information, go to *Resources* on www.commandodad.com.

- ○ Check for restrictions on baggage with your airport and your airline.
- Keep documentation on your person in one easily accessible bag.
- Pack your flight bag wisely. If possible, use a rucksack so that you have both arms free.
  - ○ Include the contents of your basic survival kit but add extra nappies and snacks. See *Chapter 5: Nutrition: An Army Marches on its Stomach* for suitable snack options.
  - ○ Depending on the time of day, take a picnic for the airport. Hungry troops are not happy troops. Remember that you cannot take fluids over 100 ml through security, but you can take sandwiches and snacks.
  - ○ Plastic spoon(s).
  - ○ If your flight includes a troop sleep, take pyjamas, special toys and any other (small) sleep triggers that your troops will appreciate.
- If you have paid for your MT to have a seat, they will have a flight bag allocation. However, only use them if you need to because troops are unable to carry/pull bags and it will fall to you to transport all luggage. This is an additional stress that you do not need.
- Dress your troops appropriately – in layers – as this will lessen the amount needed in the in-flight bag. Ensure clothes are comfortable and that your troops have a thin fleece, which may be tied around the waist until needed at altitude.
- If the queue to check your luggage is long and there is no adult to supervise the troops elsewhere, keep calm. Entertain and engage your troops by playing games that only require imagination (see *Chapter 11: Entertaining the Troops* for ideas).

- If your trooper is in a pushchair, you may not need to check it in. Most airlines (check beforehand) will let you use it until you get to the gate, and it will be waiting for you just outside the airplane door on arrival. Make sure you get baggage tags from the check-in desk, but also make your own luggage label for it.
- If you have a young BT you may be able to get a travel cot on board. It is basically a collapsible cardboard box. However, you need a bulkhead seat in order to make this a viable option (normal seats do not have the room). If you were unable to get a bulkhead seat online, get to check-in early and request one. People travelling with BTs are prime candidates for bulkhead seats.
- If your BT is breastfeeding and you wish to carry a bottle of expressed milk, check ahead with the airline.
- Many airlines now invite parents with BTs/MTs to board early via 'priority boarding'. Ask at the gate.

During the flight

- The change in pressure during take-off will cause little ears to pop. You can minimise this by having your MT/BT suck a dummy, take a drink, yawn or do an impression of a fish – depending on their stage of development.
- Accept help from cabin crew – they are the real experts on air travel with BTs. They will help you clip your BT's seat belt into yours for take-off, attach restraints for the travel cot for the flight, and even keep an eye on your BT if you need to go to the bathroom or give other troops exercise. Cabin crew will also bring hot water to make up bottles, and warm existing bottles of cold milk/expressed breast milk.

For strategies on amusing BTs/MTs during aeroplane journeys, see *Chapter 11: Entertaining the Troops*.

COMMANDO DAD TOP TIP

There are restrictions on the amount of liquids you can take in your hand baggage and containers must not hold more than 100 ml. This can cause a problem with thirsty troops. Pack empty water bottles or cups, depending on your troop's stage of development. Once you are through security you can fill the bottles or cups up with water. If there are no water fountains, buy one large bottle of water and divide it up.

COMMANDO DAD TERMS USED IN THIS CHAPTER

Base camp: home.

Basic survival kit: a bag of everyday essentials. See *Chapter 4: Kitbags: Packing Everyday Essentials* for more details.

Bimble: doing anything really slowly; used here to describe how MTs walk.

BT: baby trooper. A trooper (child) before it is mobile.

Recce: short for reconnaissance, a mission to obtain information. In this sense, working out the route.

SOP: standard operating procedure. Something that must always be done in the same way.

Yomping: a long, active walk.

CHAPTER 11:
ENTERTAINING THE TROOPS

The brief

Look lively, lads. Your troopers are your first responsibility. Entertaining and engaging them is a key skill. Bored and under-entertained troopers can change from lovely little allies into the disgruntled enemy very, very quickly. Do not let this happen.

Objective:

By the end of today's briefing you will know:

- The golden rules for entertaining the troops.
- How to entertain your troops in the house and outdoors.
- Some useful activities for troopers on the move.

★ ★ ★

A COMMANDO DAD KNOWS THE MOST ENGAGING ENTERTAINMENT TOOL IS HIS UNDIVIDED ATTENTION

The golden rules for entertaining the troops

- The most entertaining and engaging activity for BTs/MTs is your undivided attention. Any game or activity that involves you playing and enjoying time with them will be a hit. I guarantee it.

- MTs love to sing, and to be sung to. They are a forgiving audience. Brush up your vocal chords. You'll need them.

- Rely on the classics: 'Hide and Seek', 'I Spy', 'This Little Piggy', 'Round and Round the Garden' and all the other games you thought you had forgotten – but hadn't. For a reminder, go to the *Resources* section of www.commandodad.com.

- MTs that can talk will love 'spotting games'. No special equipment is required, and the variety is endless. Spot the Christmas trees, for example, or birds, or cows, or yellow cars... you get the picture.

- Don't be brainwashed into thinking your MTs need to have electronic gadgets to keep them amused. They have fantastic imaginations; help them to use them through imaginative play.

Entertaining troopers at base camp

You may not be able to be with your troopers 24 hours a day, every day. You have many tasks to perform, some of which may take you away from the unit. Do not waste your time on a negative emotion like guilt. Guilt achieves nothing. You are 100 per cent committed to being the best dad you can be. Spend your energy ensuring that you make every second with your troopers count.

Do:

- Put time aside every day to give your troopers your undivided attention.
- Give your troopers a stimulating (but safe) environment. BTs don't like pastels – parents do. Go for toys and activities with bold primary colours to capture your BT's imagination.

- Get your hands on some baby music and stories and play them regularly.
- Read to your troopers every day. It could be a baby book, the football scores, the paper, a letter.

Don't:

- Put yourself under pressure to provide entertainment to BTs. They just need to know that you are near. Just be with them and get to know each other. It's going to be a long relationship. Enjoy each other's company. Be close, talk, sing, tickle, giggle and laugh.
- Forget to chat to your troopers, however young they are. It doesn't have to be 'baby talk'. I never used it. Just use what feels comfortable for you.
- Use words you wouldn't want your MTs to repeat. They will, with startling regularity.

As your BT grows and develops, they will need more stimulation. Use your common sense. If your BT is laughing and smiling during a new activity, they are enjoying the experience. If they look upset, bewildered or are crying – and you know they're not tired, hungry, thirsty or uncomfortable – they aren't enjoying it. It's that simple.

Remember that routine is reassuring. As your BT grows they will want to explore new things but do not make too many changes all at once.

COMMANDO DAD TOP TIP

If you need to be away from base camp at bedtime, record yourself reading your trooper's favourite stories.

Fun base camp activities

There are multiple ways to entertain the troops in and around base camp

- Go into the garden, a great place to play 'spotting' and 'listening' games.
- Get noisy: sing songs or do impressions of animal noises.
- Play ball: long before an MT can throw or catch, they will enjoy rolling and holding a ball.
- Play age-appropriate puzzles together.

Even more great activities for your MTs:

- Grow plants in the garden or on the windowsill. The younger the MT, the faster the plants need to grow to keep their attention. Cress and sunflowers are good choices.
- Cooking. Older MTs will love to help in the cookhouse. Begin with easy-to-prepare favourites like bread and jam. Do not worry about the mess on the table. It can be cleaned in seconds, but your MT's sense of pleasure and achievement will last far longer.
- Play games together, like 'Building a Den', 'Hide and Seek' or 'Teddy Bears' Picnic'.
- 'Write' cards. Older MTs will love to decorate a piece of paper or a card that can be sent to relatives or friends.

Toys

A toy is simply something that a trooper uses in play and can range from a large cardboard box to the latest electronic gadget. Never feel under pressure to buy specific toys because they are in fashion. You have already given your trooper the best gift possible: your care and attention.

COMMANDO DAD TOP TIP

Troopers from birth to three years grow out of toys; they don't wear them out. This means that you can find an excellent supply of toys and activities in great condition from friends and relatives, advertised in playgroups, in the small ads, and in charity shops. Also check out Freecycle and eBay. Exercise normal levels of caution when buying.

Troopers of any age love toys with noise. Anything that lets a trooper make music will be popular, but always ensure that the 'instrument' is age-appropriate, and that your trooper does not have multiple noisy toys in play at once. It can be overstimulating for both of you.

You cannot play with multiple toys at once. They will have their favourites, and perhaps three to five extra for choice, but do not be tempted to waste space with expensive toys that your trooper does not have the time or inclination to play with.

COMMANDO DAD TOP TIP

Toy libraries are a fantastic way to ensure that your trooper has a regular supply of 'new' toys, which can be handed back when the novelty has worn thin. Find out where your nearest one is. If your trooper falls in love with a toy at the library, get this on the Christmas and birthday present lists.

If your MT gets a hoard of toys at Christmas or on their birthday, hide some of the evergreen ones: painting sets, modelling clay, colouring books, etc. These can then be brought out in the subsequent months and your MT will appreciate the 'new' toys far more. Let your MT play with the age-appropriate toys they have been given, and let them decide which ones they like. The ones that don't get played with should be kept safe and donated to charities that provide presents for underprivileged children at Christmas. There is simply nothing better that you can do with them.

TV

Television can be a wonderfully stimulating and educational tool for your trooper. It cannot, and should not, be used as a full-time carer. Limit the time your trooper spends watching TV. Daytime programming for young troopers is excellent. Check it out together.

Films

Age-appropriate films can be a great activity that MTs can share with their older siblings, and with you. They will soon let you know which are their favourite characters and films. MTs like repetition so be prepared to watch favourites many, many times. Having a few films will help your MT learn about making a choice. It also offers opportunities for role-playing games as your MT gets older (e.g. let's pretend you are Red Riding Hood).

COMMANDO DAD TOP TIP

Videotapes have fallen out of popularity and so are widely – and very cheaply – available. You can find them in some charity shops, on eBay and on Freecycle. If you have decommissioned your video player, pick one up in the small ads, or on Freecycle.

Entertaining on manoeuvres

You can improvise and adapt to any travel circumstances and still keep the troops entertained. Be prepared for all eventualities. In most forms of transport, troopers will need to be still, so you will need to learn an armoury of 'static' games.

If taking toys or activities on manoeuvres, keep them simple.

Do:

- Keep all activity items in one place, ideally in one small plastic bag in your basic survival kit.
- Take a couple of age-appropriate interactive toys for BTs. BTs love texture and gentle noise, such as rustles and squeaks (they will put everything in their mouth so avoid anything hard or sharp).

Don't:

- Take activities with a lot of small pieces – they will get lost.
- Take too much. You don't want a toy box strapped to your back.

Electronic gadgets

Electronic gadgets can entertain your MT on the move. Used sparingly, they can free you up for other tasks, including R&R. Here are some useful gadgets to have at your disposal:

- Portable DVD player and films that the MT has chosen.
- Access to your laptop. Useful for playing films and, where you can get online, it also gives access to excellent websites for MTs, often linked to their favourite TV programmes.
- MP3 player with their favourite songs and stories. Make sure it isn't too loud, or have them use earphones. Earphones are not suitable for BTs.

- Your mobile phone. You may be able to upload your MT's favourite songs and stories and have them use earphones, or put it on 'speakerphone'. Be mindful of other passengers if you are using public transport.

Be prepared with chargers. Some chargers can be plugged into the lighter outlet in your vehicle, and multiway chargers allow you to keep your satnav plugged in at the same time as other gadgets. If travelling on a coach, train or plane, check the availability of a power supply. If going overseas, make sure to purchase a worldwide plug adaptor.

Entertaining when transporting troopers by foot

Pushchairs

Ideally, have BTs facing you in their pushchair. It's reassuring for them and makes it easier for you to entertain them. Pull faces. Blow raspberries. Smile. Chat. If using interactive toys designed specifically for pushchairs, ensure that you can still collapse your pushchair with all of the toys attached.

COMMANDO DAD TOP TIP
It is not good for a BT to be strapped in to a car seat or pushchair for long periods of time. Take breaks every two hours or so on long car journeys, and, where possible on public transport, always take your BT out of their car seat or pushchair.

Entertaining when transporting troopers by car

The car is one place where interactive is not always best. Your number one concern is the safety of your troopers. Always refuse to play a game that is, or end a game that has become, distracting when driving.

COMMANDO DAD TOP TIP

As your MT gets older, have a trigger word that tells them you need them to be quiet straight away. In our car, that word is 'maps'.

BTs

- There are some excellent interactive toys available for BTs that attach to the car seat. But beware, too many can be overstimulating.
- Talking, singing and listening to favourite music or the radio are just as enjoyable as toys.

MTs

- 'Spotting games' are an excellent activity for all passengers. The most popular one in our car is 'Mini Cheddar'. Your MT gets 5 points for a yellow car, 10 points for a Mini and 25 points for a yellow Mini (a Mini Cheddar). The first one to 100 wins. Only allow one 'unconfirmed' sighting in every game, or your MT will be 'finding' yellow Minis down every side street.
- Books are engaging and, as your MT gets older, they can describe what they are looking at and 'read' to you or other passengers.
- Electronic toys can be entertaining, but make sure that they are not distracting to you. If they are, either mute them before the journey begins and provide earphones for MTs, or leave them at home.

> # COMMANDO DAD TOP TIP
> Your MT will love to throw objects as far as their strength allows. However, this activity can be dangerous and distracting in a moving vehicle. Do not give your MT a ball in the car and avoid other toys that could potentially become missiles.

Entertaining when transporting your troopers on public transport

Bus or tram

Activities on a bus or tram need to require no equipment and to happen in a confined space. Troopers love the sound of your voice. Talk to them. Singing is another great activity, especially songs that can be made as long or as short as the journey requires. 'The Wheels on the Bus' is of course the perfect choice. 'Ten Green Bottles' is another. In addition:

BTs

- Activities that involve eye-to-eye contact, e.g. 'peek-a-boo' or pulling faces.

MTs

- Activities that involve eye to eye contact, e.g. 'Peek a Boo' or pulling faces. Telling stories. Ask MTs to tell YOU a classic story.

- 'Spotting games'.

Train

For short journeys, use the same activities as you would for a bus. For longer journeys, pre-book a table, as this will give you extra space and allow you to bring along other activities.

BTs

- Take BTs out of their car seat or pushchair. Bounce them on your knee. Cuddle them close.
- Interact with them.
- Take a couple of age-appropriate interactive toys.

MTs

- Take colouring books and colouring pens or pencils, paper and playing cards.
- Check if there is a power source available. If possible, bring a portable DVD player or a laptop to show your MT their favourite film.

Aeroplane

Increasingly, airports are providing soft play areas for MTs. Check out your departure and arrival airports beforehand. If there is none available – or if they are full – be prepared with other activities.

Often, an airport will have a lot of space, but not a lot of people. If this is the case, use this empty space, while keeping your MTs under <u>close supervision</u>. Save your static games for later, when you'll need them. For example, troopers will love playing with a beach ball (which can be deflated prior to departure) and MTs will enjoy 'competitions' where you time them, e.g. 'see how long it takes you to get to that post and back', 'do five star jumps'.

- Once through security and at the gate, keep your MT close and occupied with a <u>new</u> comic or book. Do not bring old favourites, as they are irreplaceable. Do not be tempted to unpack your trooper's favourite comforter from your hand luggage (you will have packed it if the plane journey involves a sleep), as it is too important to lose.

- On the plane, especially on long-haul flights, you will often find your MTs are given an activity pack, most often involving crayons and a colouring book. There will also be excellent in-flight entertainment options and the sheer novelty of being on a plane will be hugely entertaining. However, if your MT gets bored, or nervous, your familiar static games will be engaging and reassuring.

Entertaining when out and about

You will often be out and about with your trooper. Here are some activities to enjoy:

- **The park**: feed the ducks, have a picnic, jump in the leaves (or puddles or snowdrifts if your MT has the right kit), go on the swings and the slide, play with a ball, meet other troopers, etc.

- **Libraries**: join your local library. It is never too early to introduce your trooper to books, and libraries have fantastic sections for troopers, and other activities such as storytelling groups. Wherever you travel in the UK, you will be reasonably close to a library.

- **Museums**: modern museums offer engaging, interactive activities for MTs, and are often free of charge. Check out your local museum and, as with libraries, it is a good activity to have in the bag for when you are away from home.

- **Swimming**: swimming is an essential life skill and introducing your MT to water is a great opportunity for them to gain confidence. It is also great fun. Sign up for classes now.

- **Fun days out**: zoos, castles, woods, petting farms. Check out your area in your local paper or online. You might be surprised what's on offer and the free activities available.

COMMANDO DAD TOP TIP

MTs will enjoy doing familiar things in new places. Do they like feeding the ducks? Take them to a new park to do it in. If you normally drive to the playgroup, take the bus, or walk.

Entertaining in the great outdoors

The opportunities for outdoor activities are endless, because all they require is outdoor space and imagination. Outdoor activities are enjoyable, burn energy, teach teamwork, keep MTs entertained and are cheap or free. I highly recommend them.

The golden rules for outdoor adventures

- Be safe. Keep your BTs and MTs under your constant surveillance.
- Be fully engaged with your MTs.
- Do age-appropriate activities.
- Ideally, carry out a thorough recce before taking your troops on an outdoor activity.
- Take extra snacks for refs as your MTs will work up an appetite.
- Get them kitted up appropriately, as being cold and wet is bad for morale.
- Either drive to your destination or make it a short walk away. Yomping to or from a destination can be exhausting for MTs.

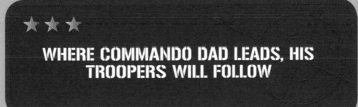

★ ★ ★

WHERE COMMANDO DAD LEADS, HIS TROOPERS WILL FOLLOW

Outdoor activities for MTs

There are two types of outdoor activity that MTs will enjoy:

Foraging: where you go out to find materials that can be used to make something back at base camp. Here are some good examples to get you started:

- Art supplies: Take your MTs into the great outdoors with a small bag (do not take a huge bag as it will get filled) and ask them to pick up leaves, sticks, seeds, acorns, flowers, etc. that you will use to make a picture when you get home. This activity is about finding things that have fallen to the ground, **not** picking things off plants, trees or bushes.
- Nature wristband: A surprisingly fun activity that only requires a roll of adhesive tape. Make each MT a 'bracelet' using the tape, sticky side up, and ask them to find little items that you can help them stick to it. Snip the wristband off when you get home and use it to recount the day's activities, and to display it (the fridge door is a good place).

Skills-based: where you use a fun activity to teach your MTs important skills such as observation, listening and following instructions. Here are some good examples to get you started:

- Pathfinding: use items that have fallen to the ground to make simple markers. The best are arrows made from twigs as they can show a change in direction. It's also possible to make cairns (little piles of stones). You then use your own markers to make your way back to your starting point.
- Follow the troop leader: You start as the troop leader and ask your MTs to follow what you do. Use the space. Run around trees, hop, skip and jump. Let your MTs take it in turns to be the leader. An extension of this can be asking MTs to follow the leader's spoken instructions: 'Run on the spot!', 'Hop on one leg!', etc.

COMMANDO DAD TOP TIP

Ensure that MTs know they must NEVER eat any berries, seeds, mushrooms or fungi that you pick up when foraging.

Entertaining on shopping trips

If at all possible, leave all but the littlest BTs at home. It can be a challenging mission, even for you. If your MT is with you, the best way to keep them engaged is to involve them in the task at hand. As ever, be prepared with an excellent shopping list that will help make the sortie as short as possible.

- Always take a trolley and have your trooper in it (even if you only need a few items). Most supermarkets either have a trolley that will enable you to secure your car seat, or have moulded basic seats designed for BTs.
- With MTs, hand them (non-breakable and light) items and ask them to put them in the trolley.
- Ask them to find items they will recognise – bananas for example.
- Colour spot – give them a colour and they have to find as many objects as possible of that colour as you move around the shop.

COMMANDO DAD TOP TIP

Decide beforehand if MTs will be allowed 'treats' such as chocolate or a comic. And then stand firm. Do not go against your better judgement when the complaining gets too much, even if your MT is on 'permanent send'. If you do, you will have taught your MT a very important lesson. They can have whatever they want, but only if they really, really, really whine first.

Playgroups

Playgroups are an excellent way to entertain the troops. They give your troopers a safe area to play, a different environment to explore, and new friends to meet. It will give you the opportunity to meet other parents and carers, which will have a positive effect on self-esteem and morale (see *Chapter 7: Morale: A Commando Dad's Secret Weapon*).

COMMANDO DAD TOP TIP

It's important to give MTs opportunities to play independently. Don't be afraid to take a step back. You'll be surprised what your MTs come up with and what they can do.

MTs love to play with each other. It helps teach them about themselves and the world. However, it is not until MTs are about two years old that they want to play and interact with other MTs consistently. Sometimes they will play with each other, sometimes they won't. Don't push them.

Don't waste energy feeling nervous if you are the only man at a playgroup. You have the most important thing in the world in common: you are all parents.

COMMANDO DAD TERMS USED IN THIS CHAPTER

Base camp: home.

Basic survival kit: a bag of everyday essentials. See *Chapter 4: Kitbags: Packing Everyday Essentials* for more details.

BT: baby trooper. A trooper (child) before it is mobile.

Cookhouse: kitchen.

MT: mobile trooper. A trooper that can shuffle, crawl, stand up and, eventually, walk.

Permanent send: the experience of having your MT talking at you non-stop, seemingly without pausing for breath.

R&R: rest and recuperation.

Recce: short for reconnaissance, a mission to obtain information. In this sense, checking something out beforehand.

Refs: refreshment break.

Sortie: a trip away from base camp.

Unit: family.

Yomping: a long, active walk.

CHAPTER 12:
DEALING WITH HOSTILITIES

The brief:
Conflict is an inevitable part of life. One of the best ways to avoid it, or minimise its impact, is to establish firm boundaries and good discipline in the unit.

Objective:
By the end of today's briefing you will have a greater understanding of:

- The importance of establishing boundaries.
- Discipline: what it is, when and how to use it.
- Unit regulations: setting rules.
- Hand grenades: tantrums and how to deal with them.
- Battle fatigue and how to avoid it.
- How to deal with hostilities with the calmness and leadership befitting a Commando Dad.

Establishing boundaries

Boundaries are the limits that are deemed acceptable in your unit. They are underpinned by rules – and consequences.

It is a myth that MTs don't like boundaries. They need them because they give them security and something to push against. Without boundaries, your MTs will ultimately feel insecure.

Boundaries need to be clear and consistently implemented. Everyone in the unit – including adults – must operate within the same boundaries.

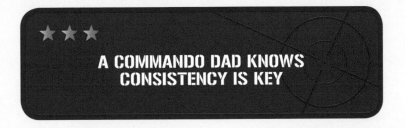

★ ★ ★

A COMMANDO DAD KNOWS CONSISTENCY IS KEY

You need to be consistent in every area of your parenting, for everyone's sake. If you are not consistent, both you and your MT will feel unsettled, confused and frustrated. Consistently work to be the best parent you can be.

COMMANDO DAD TOP TIP

Consistency is key, but that does not mean that you have to consistently do something that isn't working. You need to find what works for you and your troopers, and stick to it. If that stops working, change it. There is no one set of strategies that all parents can consistently follow when bringing up troopers. It's all about trial and error. Mistakes are great because you will learn from them and hone your skills as an effective dad.

Discipline

Discipline is the act of teaching your MTs to obey rules, and using age-appropriate sanctions to guide behaviour. Its purpose is to keep your MTs safe, and to teach and guide them. It is not about punishment. Discipline begins by establishing unit regulations, or family rules.

Unit Regulations

Your MT, even up until the age of three, has a very limited vocabulary. Therefore, when setting rules remember:

Do:

- Use touch, body language and tone of voice as ways of non-verbal communication.
- Maintain eye contact to engage your MT.
- Always be the model of behaviour that you want your MT to emulate.

Don't:

- Use too many words.
- Set too many rules.
- Confuse your MT with conflicting signals: e.g. telling them not to do something but laughing; saying something is OK when your body language shows that you are angry.

For BTs:

BTs are too young for discipline. BTs under one year are too young to grasp the concept of cause and effect.

- Do lay the foundation for later discipline by using 'no' when the BT is engaged in a potentially unsafe or undesirable activity, and a visual cue, such as wagging a finger.

- Always provide an alternative toy/activity to distract them.
- Always praise your BT for good behaviour.
- Use the 'out of sight, out of mind' approach: your BT is naturally inquisitive. Keep objects that you don't want your BT to play with hidden away and out of reach. Baby proof your home. For information and tips, see *Chapter 1: The Advance Party: Preparing Base Camp*.

For MTs:

MTs between the ages of one and three are better able to understand cause and effect, but still do not have the ability to think logically. Follow the steps below to lay the groundwork for later, logical decision-making:

Do:

- Keep calm and remain objective when disciplining your MT.
- Use a firm, calm voice.
- Use the word 'no' only when you mean it.
- Use age-appropriate sanctions; see below for some ideas.

Don't:

- Use discipline to vent anger or frustration.
- Debate or argue the point with your MT. 'No' means 'no' (so make sure you mean it).
- Pay attention to your MT only when they display bad behaviour.

COMMANDO DAD TOP TIP

It is very easy to make the word 'no' your default response to requests – even reasonable ones. If you initially deny a request and then relent, you teach your MT that sometimes 'no' means 'yes'. This is confusing for MTs, and undermines discipline. Say 'no' only when you mean it and follow through.

Use a variety of approaches for discipline. You should have an effective 'scale' of measures that are incrementally more serious, and you will find some ideas below. The top of that scale should NEVER be smacking your troopers.

Hitting shows a distinct lack of self-discipline. It is not appropriate behaviour.

- If you 'solve' conflict by hitting your trooper, you teach them that conflict resolution begins with physical violence. This robs them of the ability to develop vital life skills, such as reasoning, compromise and adaptability.
- Escalation becomes a problem. If you start with smacking, where will you go next?

★ ★ ★

A COMMANDO DAD IS RESPECTED – NOT FEARED – BY HIS TROOPERS

Age-appropriate sanctions

Design a cue that works with your MT. A squeeze of the hand, a stern look or a pointed finger can all be very effective methods for alerting your MT that their behaviour is inappropriate and will not be tolerated.

- The first weapon in your discipline armoury is 'The Look' – a stern, disapproving frown that MTs of every age will understand.
- If your MT is doing something that is harmful to themselves or others, immediately remove them from the situation.

- If your MT does not have eye contact with you but is doing something that you need to stop immediately, shout 'STOP' or 'HEY' – any short word will do. The shock of hearing you suddenly raise your voice is alarming and will stop them in their tracks. Then remove them from the situation if you need to.

COMMANDO DAD TOP TIP

Raising your voice is a disciplinary tactic. If you shout at your MT regularly, it ceases to be an effective strategy.

- ROPs: restriction of privileges. Start to teach your MT that bad behaviour has consequences, but remain positive. So, rather than say 'Naughty MTs don't get to visit granddad', say 'Granddad would love a visit from a good little MT, but naughty little MTs would have to stay at base camp'.
- From three years old, 'time out', where MTs are moved to a designated spot, and deprived of your attention, starts to be an effective disciplinary strategy. We found that using the following rule of thumb worked for us: one minute for every year of your MT's age. Every time the MT leaves the 'naughty spot', 'time out' starts again.

★ ★ ★

A COMMANDO DAD CONSTRUCTIVELY CRITICISES BEHAVIOUR, NEVER HIS TROOPERS.

COMMANDO DAD TOP TIP

Never criticise your MT, only their actions. So, for example, say 'That was selfish behaviour', not 'You are selfish'. Be aware that your MT looks to you for guidance on who they are. Use that power wisely.

Everyone makes mistakes. Discipline is no different. The important thing is to apologise to your MT if you feel they were disciplined too harshly.

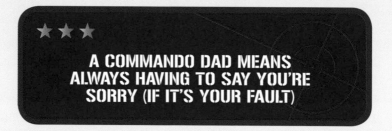

★ ★ ★

A COMMANDO DAD MEANS ALWAYS HAVING TO SAY YOU'RE SORRY (IF IT'S YOUR FAULT)

You must lead by example. If you expect your MT to apologise when they have done something wrong, then you must set the example. MTs may be young, but they have the full range of human emotions and a heartfelt apology will have the same effect on them that it would have on you. Even when they are in the wrong – and your discipline was appropriate – it never hurts to ensure that your MT knows they are loved and cared for. Never go to sleep on an argument.

You will probably not be the only one in your base camp that has the authority to discipline your MT – for example, your wife or partner, your parents and your in-laws may also be responsible for discipline. Ensure that you are all consistent and share one set of strategies. If there is a 'weak link' in the discipline chain (i.e. an adult that can be relied upon not to use discipline), your MTs will find and exploit it.

COMMANDO DAD TOP TIP

You must maintain harmony in the unit to avoid battle fatigue, the sense of exhaustion that comes from living in an environment of constant arguing. This can be very bad for morale and impact your effectiveness as a parent. To find out more about the importance of morale, see *Chapter 7: Morale: A Commando Dad's Secret Weapon*.

MT tantrums: what they are and how, and when, to deal with them

What is a tantrum?

A tantrum is the hand grenade of the behavioural world. It is an extreme and uncontrolled outburst of anger and frustration from your MT. It will be physical – e.g. flailing arms and legs, rolling on the ground, banging heads, hitting – and very, very loud. An MT lobs them from about 18 months to at least four years old. Expect tantrums to become less frequent – and less explosive – as your MT gets older and can express their needs through language.

Tantrums are inevitable. They are your MT's way of dealing with anger and frustration: big emotions that they are learning to get to grips with. The triggers for tantrums generally fall into three categories.

- Asking an MT to do something they don't want to do.
- Stopping an MT from doing something they do want to do.
- Saying 'no' to something the MT wants.

Avoiding tantrums

Learn to recognise when your MT is about to pull the tantrum pin and take evasive action.

Do:

- Be the model of behaviour that you want your MT to emulate.
- Learn to recognise your MT's tantrum cues early. Take evasive action. Distraction techniques work well.
- Praise your MT's good behaviour. You may want to create a reward chart for this, or download one from the *Resources* section of www.commandodad.com.

Don't:

- Let your MT get too hungry, tired or bored. This can create fertile ground for tantrums.
- Escalate the situation by getting angry. Keep calm and in control.
- Plead with your MT for cooperation. They need to know that you are in control.

COMMANDO DAD TOP TIP

Don't give in to demands in order to stop a tantrum. This will teach your MT to throw tantrums in order to get what they want. And they will.

Dealing with tantrums

The most effective way to deal with a tantrum that has begun, or is about to begin, is the distraction technique. MTs have very short attention spans. Make this work in your favour.

Key distraction techniques:

- **Entertain**: make it an SOP to take a (small) bag of decoy objects on sorties away from the unit. You need something to keep their minds, and hands, busy. The most effective thing I used was a box of plasters, but you could use any small toy, such as a rattle or 'buggy book'.

- **Role play**: surprise your MT out of their tantrum by acting out of character or doing something surprising. I found pretending to cry – very loudly and theatrically – would often make my MT laugh and could change the mood instantly. Find out what works for your MT.

- **Engage**: make an alternative suggestion for something to do, and do it together, immediately.

Mounting a rescue operation

Your MT may be hostage to their own emotions and behaviour. They simply don't know how to stop and recover the situation. That is why you must always stay calm and give them an 'out'. Don't make it personal. I have found it effective to say 'Shall we start again?' and actually pretend to rewind the situation, complete with comedy sound effects. If you give your MTs a good option, they are likely to take it.

When a tantrum is in full swing

When tantrums explode, deal with them with the calmness befitting a Commando Dad.

Do:

- Keep calm and take control of the situation. If at base camp, put them in a safe area to calm down. If in public, remove them from the situation.

- Make sure that your MT is safe.

Don't:

- Leave your MTs unattended in a public place, in order to show them that you are 'ignoring' their bad behaviour.

- Try to communicate with your MT during a tantrum. It needs to run its course.

The aftermath

Speak to your MT calmly about the tantrum afterwards. Be understanding and kind, but ensure they understand that tantrum behaviour is not acceptable at home or in public. The best long-term way to deal with MT tantrums is to create firm boundaries and stick to them. This teaches MTs that lobbing tantrum hand grenades is not an effective strategy.

COMMANDO DAD TOP TIP

If your MT's tantrums are increasing in frequency, intensity or duration, and you have any concerns, consult your doctor.

Dealing with conflict: public hostilities

Sometimes, regardless of the fact that your troops are well behaved and operating within reasonable noise levels, you may encounter hostility from the general public.

In public, you will need to:

- Assess the situation (often):
  - Are you confident that you are in control and doing everything possible to keep the troops entertained and well behaved?
  - Are the troops operating within reasonable noise levels?
- If the answer to any of the questions above is 'no' (and there are no unusual circumstances, e.g. your trooper is ill, teething or overtired) then immediately take control of the situation and calmly restore order. See *Chapter 11: Entertaining the Troops* for ideas for activities to engage your troops.
- If the answer to the questions above is 'yes', maintain your stiff upper lip. Sometimes people are unreasonable. Rise above it. Where the hostility

is passive (eye-rolling and tutting, etc.), ignore it. Where you are directly approached, explain the situation calmly. Do not let other people's unreasonable behaviour make you angry or agitated. This will upset the troops.

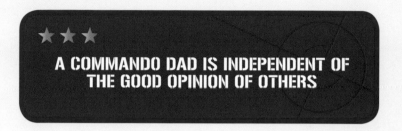

★ ★ ★

A COMMANDO DAD IS INDEPENDENT OF THE GOOD OPINION OF OTHERS

- In either instance do not lose control and shout at your MTs to keep strangers happy.
- If your MTs see you being more concerned with the feelings of strangers, they will 'learn' that they are not as important to you as random, unreasonable members of the public. This is not true.
- Do not lose control and shout at members of the public. Be reasonable and rational.
- Troopers learn how to deal with situations by watching how you deal with them. Make them – and yourself – proud.

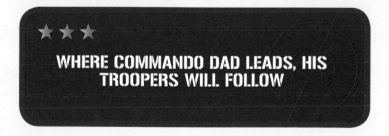

★ ★ ★

WHERE COMMANDO DAD LEADS, HIS TROOPERS WILL FOLLOW

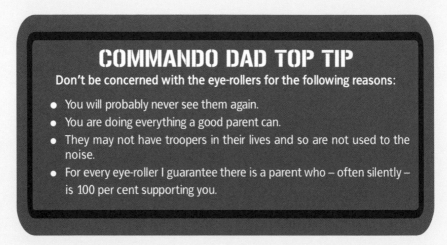

COMMANDO DAD TOP TIP

Don't be concerned with the eye-rollers for the following reasons:

- You will probably never see them again.
- You are doing everything a good parent can.
- They may not have troopers in their lives and so are not used to the noise.
- For every eye-roller I guarantee there is a parent who – often silently – is 100 per cent supporting you.

Dissension in the ranks: dealing with hostility between you and your MT

There are infinite reasons why there may be conflict between you and your troopers.

★ ★ ★

LEARN TO IMPROVISE, ADAPT AND OVERCOME

- Take deep breaths and keep calm. Conflict cannot be solved effectively if you are angry.
- Ask the MT what the problem is. Do not expect a rational or reasonable explanation, as your MT may not have acquired these skills (yet). It is your job to teach them these skills and it is an ongoing process. This is a good place to start.

- Listen to the answer and demonstrate that you have listened and understood. Do not criticise their reasoning; to a young MT it is common sense, for example, to continue an activity that they enjoy.
- Avoid escalation into angry confrontation. Do not get drawn into arguments with your MT. You are an elite dad. Act like one.
- Take responsibility. Where you are partly to blame, accept responsibility.
- If your MT is in physical danger – e.g. having a tantrum near a road, or any other potentially hazardous area – immediately remove them physically from that situation and begin the conflict resolution steps above.

Remember, at all times:

★ ★ ★

A COMMANDO DAD KEEPS CALM UNDER PRESSURE

'Flash to bang' time

Many factors can affect 'flash to bang' time – i.e. the time between stimulus (your trooper's behaviour) and your response. These include tiredness, hunger and frustration. A major contributing factor is 'compassion fatigue', where you just do not feel you have an ounce of compassion left to see things from your MT's point of view. Take a deep breath and dig deep. If your 'bang' is louder at some times more than others, it can be confusing and unsettling for troopers. Remember, consistency is key. Learn what shortens your 'det cord' (i.e. what makes you lose your temper) and take evasive action.

Do not let hostilities break out because of your (over)reaction to events. For example, if your MT breaks something, ask yourself how you would react if a guest in your house had done the same. Your reaction to your MT should be equally as understanding. However, if your MT breaks something outside your own home (e.g. in someone else's house, a supermarket, a playgroup) the appropriate steps are:

- Immediately take responsibility and clean up the mess.
- Offer to pay and/or replace.
- If your MT is old enough to understand the concept of manners, find an appropriate adult to whom they can apologise.
- If it is appropriate for you to speak further to your MT about the incident, do so in private (but avoid threatening phrases such as 'Just wait until I get you home.'). Do not embarrass your MT by reprimanding them in public for minor offences. Public reprimands should be used when the lesson is so important that it cannot wait: for example, running out onto a road, physical fighting, throwing objects.

Underlying causes of conflict

- **Frustration**: Learn to understand it. For example, being strapped in a seat while someone that you can't communicate with spoon-feeds you something that you may, or may not, enjoy is not going to be a thrilling experience.
- **Tiredness**: Never, ever underestimate the power of lack of sleep. Learn to recognise its negative effects in yourself, too.
- **Physical illness**: Always treat your troopers with compassion, but especially when they are ill.
- **Pushing against boundaries**: Accept that pushing against boundaries is a natural part of development. It is not a personal attack.
- **Hunger:** A hungry MT is an unhappy MT. Learn to recognise your MT's hunger cues, stick to scheduled mealtimes and keep healthy snacks to hand.

Learn to recognise the triggers in your own MT, and devise strategies to avoid or lessen the impact where possible. Remember: sometimes there is no 'solution' and whatever you do will have no effect. In these situations, keep them safe, yourself calm, and ride it out.

COMMANDO DAD TERMS USED IN THIS CHAPTER

Base camp: home.
Battle fatigue: a sense of exhaustion and frustration that comes from living in an environment of constant arguing.
BT: baby trooper. A trooper (child) before it is mobile.
Compassion fatigue: a feeling at the end of the day when tiredness makes you feel that you have no compassion left. Dig deep.
Det cord: the detonation cord that sets off the explosive. A short det cord means a short 'flash to bang' time.
'Flash to bang' time: the time between stimulus (your troopers' behaviour) and your response.
Lob: throw.
MT: mobile trooper. A trooper that can shuffle, crawl, stand up and, eventually, walk.
ROPs: restriction of privileges.
SOP: standard operating procedure. Something that must always be done in the same way.

PASSING OUT CEREMONY

Congratulations, gentlemen. You have reached the end of your basic training manual. You are now equipped with the basic skills that you need to be a Commando Dad.

At the beginning of this manual, I spoke about a dad falling somewhere between Hero, Role Model and Protector. I believe that the information and guidance I have given you in this book will help, but ultimately, you have decided to step into those shoes.

You will have supplemented the guidance provided here with a lot of practical experience, and gained confidence in your own skills.

But remember that elite forces are continually training, honing and learning new skills. As a Commando Dad, you must do likewise. Keep this book close and refer to it often.

COMMANDO DAD

Below, I have listed the rules that appear throughout this manual as a reminder of the elite standards you are working towards and operating at.

A COMMANDO DAD IS A HANDS-ON DAD

A COMMANDO DAD KNOWS THAT PREPARATION AND PLANNING PREVENT POOR PARENTAL PERFORMANCE

A COMMANDO DAD TAKES HIS RESPONSIBILITIES SERIOUSLY

A COMMANDO DAD HAS HIS KITBAG SQUARED AWAY, READY FOR REDEPLOYMENT

A COMMANDO DAD WILL IMPROVISE, ADAPT AND OVERCOME

A COMMANDO DAD LEADS BY EXAMPLE

A COMMANDO DAD ALWAYS ACTS IN THE BEST INTERESTS OF HIS TROOPERS

A COMMANDO DAD ENSURES GOOD ROUTINES ARE STANDARD OPERATING PROCEDURE IN HIS UNIT

A COMMANDO DAD REGULARLY EVALUATES HIS PERFORMANCE AND MAKES ADJUSTMENTS ACCORDINGLY

A COMMANDO DAD CANNOT HELP THE WAY HE FEELS BUT HE CAN HELP THE WAY HE ACTS A COMMANDO DAD WILL TAKE CARE OF HIS UNIT WITH ALL MEANS AT HIS DISPOSAL

A COMMANDO DAD PUTS THE SAFETY OF HIS TROOPS AT THE HEART OF ALL TRAVEL PLANS

A COMMANDO DAD KNOWS THE MOST ENGAGING ENTERTAINMENT TOOL IS HIS UNDIVIDED ATTENTION

WHERE COMMANDO DAD LEADS, HIS TROOPERS WILL FOLLOW

A COMMANDO DAD KNOWS CONSISTENCY IS KEY

A COMMANDO DAD IS RESPECTED – NOT FEARED – BY HIS TROOPERS

A COMMANDO DAD CONSTRUCTIVELY CRITICISES BEHAVIOUR, NEVER HIS TROOPERS

A COMMANDO DAD MEANS ALWAYS HAVING TO SAY YOU'RE SORRY (IF IT'S YOUR FAULT)

A COMMANDO DAD IS INDEPENDENT OF THE GOOD OPINION OF OTHERS

A COMMANDO DAD KEEPS CALM UNDER PRESSURE

Finally, I too am a Commando Dad in training. If you have any experiences or advice that would help me on my journey, please share them with me – and other dads – at www.commandodad.com.

Fall out, Commando Dads.

GLOSSARY

AWOL: Absent without leave; used to describe troopers leaving the table without permission.

BT: Baby trooper. A trooper (child) before it is mobile.

Base camp: Home.

Base-camp admin: Housework.

Basic survival kit: A bag of everyday essentials. See *Chapter 4: Kitbags: Packing Everyday Essentials* for more details.

Battle fatigue: A sense of exhaustion and frustration that comes from living in an environment of constant arguing. Bad for morale.

Bimble: Doing anything really slowly; used here to describe how MTs walk.

Bomb disposal: Emptying dirty nappies into outside bins every night.

Compassion fatigue: A feeling at the end of the day when tiredness makes you feel that you have no compassion left. Dig deep.

Cookhouse: Kitchen.

Det cord: The detonation cord that sets off an explosion. A short det cord means a short 'flash to bang' time.

'Flash to bang' time: The time it takes between stimulus (your trooper's behaviour) and your response. 'Flash to bang' time gets shorter the more tired you are, or the more stressful the situation becomes.

G10 Store: A place in base camp where you store all of the essential equipment.

Howitzer: A gun that uses a comparatively small charge to propel projectiles at relatively high trajectories. Here used to describe the explosive contents of a nappy.

KFS: Knife, fork, spoon; cutlery.

Light-order missions: Short sorties away from base camp. Visiting the shops, a playgroup or the park, for example.

Lob: Throw.

Long-term major deployment: Holidays.

Mid-term deployment: Extended times away from base camp, such as long car or train journeys, or flights.

MT: Mobile trooper. A trooper that can shuffle, crawl, stand up and, eventually, walk.

Mufti: Non-uniform; plain clothes.

Nocturnal missions: Any activity that happens after 'lights out'.

Negligent discharge: When you accidentally fire a round when you weren't meant to. In this instance, it is used to describe the ability of a BT to pee or poo the moment their nappy is removed.

0-silly-hundred-hours: Very early, too early, in the morning.

Permanent send: The experience of having your MT talking at you non-stop, seemingly without pausing for breath.

Personal admin: Shower, shave and shampoo.

Recce: Short for reconnaissance, a mission to obtain information.

Refs: Refreshment break.

Reveille: A call to wake up personnel; used to describe the morning routine.

ROPs: Restriction of privileges. A punishment.

R&R: Rest and recuperation.

Silent running: Continuing to operate normally, but in silence or near silence (as used on submarines). Used to describe the quietness needed in the early days of having a BT in the house.

Sortie: The dispatch of the unit; used to describe a trip away from base camp.

Squared away: Everything organised and in the right place.

SOP: Standard operating procedures; the normal, acknowledged way of doing things.

Sympathetic detonation: An unintended detonation, caused by a nearby explosion. Used to describe the chain reaction of emotions set off by you.

Thunderbox: Toilet.

Unit: Family. Includes your own children and those you care for, partners and other carers.

Up to speed: Where all relevant information, and the mission and actions to carry out, are clear.

US: 'Unserviceable', i.e. broken or not fit for purpose.

Yomping: A long, active walk.

INDEX

COMMANDO DAD'S NOTES

COMMANDO DAD'S NOTES

COMMANDO DAD'S NOTES

COMMANDO DAD'S NOTES

COMMANDO DAD'S NOTES